Charles Fierro
In His Own Words

What readers say about *Charles Fierro In His Own Words*

"This book is a treasure trove for lovers of music and opens the door to anyone who is interested in exploring and learning. Each article is a gem of insight, wisdom and clarity, expressed with eloquence and elegance in vivid descriptive language that brings the subject to life."—*Linda Love, Pianist, teacher, poet.*

"This book is pure Charles, erudite, enlightening, inspiring, warm, elegant, passionate, connecting concepts and ideas from diverse fields as only a razor-sharp mind can...written in a clear, charming, concise and understated manner. I could not put it down. A most welcome must-read for teachers and students alike." —*Dr. Wojciech Kocyan, Clinical Professor of Music, Loyola Marymount University, Los Angeles.*

"What a privilege to read this book! I found myself frequently nodding in agreement and marveling at his choice of the most vivid and significant examples followed by just the perfect words. Insightful! Bravo!"—*Nancy Arnold, Piano Teacher, Vocal Coach, Board member Music Teachers' Association, West Los Angeles Branch.*

"I love 'hearing' Charles Fierro's voice again in his essays. Charles asked that we perform Guillaume Lekeu's violin sonata. Those rehearsals and discussions about a multitude of topics are cherished.The tributes to Charles accurately describe an exceptional artist. We should remember his talents and intellect, his enthusiasm and empathy." —*Jacqueline Suzuki, Violinist.*

"These essays are filled with the humanity and talent characteristic of Charles Fierro. Despite the diverse range the common denominator is the love of music, pedagogy and life. Charles Fierro prizes imagination and insight as keys to creativity. Clearly he has these in abundance. This book is a pleasure to read."—*Katherine Kiefer, Music lover.*

"A work full of wonder and inspiration, one which can only have been written by a prodigious musician endowed with both a superb intellect and a truly remarkable heart." —*Antoinette Perry, Concert Artist, Professor of Practice, University of Southern California, Thornton School of Music.*

"A delicious peek into the life, mind and musical world of SoCal pianist Charles Fierro through his writings and the eyes of his colleagues and students. I found this generous sharing to be expanding, encouraging, wise and even practical."—*Elreen Bower, Music lover.*

"Concise yet comprehensive, these irreplaceable writings by musical luminary Charles Fierro should be required reading for all pianists and students of music. With characteristic clarity, Fierro conveys unique insights on topics ranging from major composers (many of whom he knew) to questions of pedagogy and philosophy, all based on his own vast experience. Vivid, context-building reactions by students and colleagues complement Fierro's sparkling prose. Together, the work stands as a reminder of the lives he touched, and a worthy introduction to future generations."—*Steven Niles, Concert Artist and Professor, Los Angeles City College.*

Nothing is better than music. When it takes us out of time, it has done more for us than we have the right to hope for.

—Nadia Boulanger

Charles Fierro In His Own Words

Edited by Mary A. Hannon

Charles Fierro In His Own Words

Publisher: Nancy C. Fierro

Editor: Mary A. Hannon

Book Design: Kathy Weaver

Copy Editing: Carol Gee

Logo Design: LogoDesign.net

For more information, contact:
charlesfierrobook@icloud.com

ISBN-978-0-578-95860-6

About the Editor

Mary A. Hannon served as writer, editor and publisher of *Piano Forte*, a quarterly newsletter for pianists and music lovers to share useful information, ideas and personal experience. Over a twenty-year period her articles and interviews filled the pages of every publication. She also edited and published *Piano Talk, Conversations with Stewart Gordon*. Mary serves on the board of Piano Spheres and the Sara Compinsky Master Class and continues to consult with individuals and organizations on the publication of newsletters and printed programs. She is an amateur pianist and lives in South Pasadena, California.

Contents

Preface

Charles Fierro was an enthusiastic contributor to *Piano Forte*, a newsletter that I published from 1998 to 2018. His first article appeared in 1999 and was titled "Turning the Tables". In the years that followed, he contributed twenty-five articles, the final one being about composer Guillaume Lekeu in 2017. His articles spanned the life of the publication and were of popular appeal to readers. As editor, what struck me most about his work was how well he could express ideas in just a few words. Each article, concise and luminous, a pearl of insight. I decided to share them with a wider audience in this book.

Part I of the book consists of his body of articles. They shine light on the joy of his life as a musician. He introduces us to a few chosen musicians that influenced him and follows with his thoughts on a wide array of subjects of importance in his career as teacher, performer, recording artist and adjudicator. As evidenced in his writings, Charles was a brilliant musician and keen observer of life, gifts he graciously shared with others. Part II offers touching recollections by colleagues and students who came into Charles' orbit and were influenced by him.

With heartfelt appreciation, I will be forever grateful to Charles for his interest and generosity in contributing this collection of articles to *Piano Forte,* and it is with enthusiasm that I offer them to you in these pages. I hope that the contents of this book will not only enrich and entertain you but that you will uncover here some pearls of your own.

I wish to thank Dr. Nancy Fierro for her significant support and contribution to the book. Her input and suggestions all along were valuable essentials throughout the entire process of bringing this publication to fruition. Special thanks to Dr. Dmitry Rachmanov for contributing the Foreword and back cover summary to *Charles Fierro In His Own Words.* I am grateful too, for his enthusiastic encouragement while the book was in progress. Appreciation to Carol Gee who generously offered her eye-for-detail proofreading skills and creative insight to this project. Kathy Weaver of Kathy Weaver Design provided her expertise and advice on graphic design, formatting and publishing. Her skill and creativity are greatly appreciated.

Mary A. Hannon
South Pasadena, California
June 14, 2021

Foreword

Dr. Charles Fierro was a multifaceted musician with an extraordinary scope of interests and breadth of knowledge: a fine performer and a recording artist who brought to light many lesser-known works, granting them their second lives; a lecturer who researched off-the-beaten-track topics and shared them with his audiences with true passion; an inspirational educator, master class clinician, an adjudicator, an author. . .the list goes on.

This book presents Dr. Fierro's collected essays extracted from his years as a contributing writer to the *Piano Forte* newsletter, published by Mary A. Hannon from 1998 to 2018. In his writings, he explores a wide variety of musical subjects, personae, styles, and issues facing musicians in their careers and daily work. This book will be of interest to musicians and music lovers alike.

I was fortunate to know and interact with Dr. Fierro. My first meeting with him took place during my initial visit to California State University, Northridge (CSUN) for my job interview in March of 2007. After my interview recital and master class, Charles greeted me, introducing himself and showing his support. His words and his whole persona exuded goodwill, enthusiasm and warmth. The bond of our friendship and professional collaboration was established then, and it continued for the next ten years until his passing.

By the time of our first encounter, it had been several years since Charles' retirement from CSUN. Yet his connection to the school where he had taught for thirty years (1970-2000) was still very strong. As a Professor Emeritus, Dr. Fierro continued to perform occasional solo faculty recitals and collaborate with his erstwhile colleagues.

He also attended and supported other faculty and guest artist recitals. Occasionally he would write a review of the recitals he had attended (some of which are included in this collection). He remained an ardent supporter of the CSUN piano program. Every year in December and in May, Dr. Fierro would invariably sit in on our end-of-the-semester juries of our piano majors. His comments and recommendations were right on the mark. Without necessarily knowing the individual student backgrounds, he could pinpoint their strengths and weaknesses with his laser-sharp ears, and provide constructive recommendations based on his musical intuition and vast experience. He truly cared about students. Young at heart, Charles always felt rejuvenated being around young people. Every spring semester he would substitute as a guest master class clinician for our weekly Piano Master Class course, never accepting an honorarium for his work. His teaching was always inspirational to students, opening up new horizons for them in their work on the piano masterworks at hand. After the class, I would invariably hear Dr. Fierro's detailed postmortem report on every student performance he had heard that day. In our follow-up conversations, he enthusiastically discussed the music that was performed, the students and the best way to help them.

His unbridled enthusiasm for art and culture, be that an art exhibit, a book he had read, a new composer he had discovered, or a performance of a great artist he had attended, always elicited vivid reactions on his part, fed by his deep passion for all things artistic, his child-like curiosity and insatiable thirst for knowledge. Charles studied French in the last couple years of his life. An enthusiastic student, he was also learning Armenian and was able to speak it quite well with his Armenian neighbors in Glendale, California.

All these aspects of Dr. Fierro's professional persona, his probing intellect and his gifts as a storyteller, found their eloquent expressions in his writings. We are fortunate to have them as part of his legacy, for they are original, thought-provoking and stimulating. He was a true wordsmith, his prose unfolding with lucidity, words and sentences conveying the points he was making succinctly.

Among the collected articles, the reader will find essays and memoirs on composers that Charles championed, advocated for, collaborated with, or may have had personal recollections of, such as Aaron Copland, Ingolf Dahl, Paul Hindemith, Edward MacDowell or Guillaume Lekeu. You will also find Fierro's concert reviews of performers as well as some composers, which may have been less known at the time of writing. Another type of article in the book touches upon philosophical topics, reflections on musicians' issues, such as daily practice vs public performance "Turning the Tables", memorization "To Memorize or Not", a teacher and a pupil "Listen to Your Teacher", or experiences of a competition judge "Confessions of an Adjudicator". In these pieces, Charles' comments are most original and witty. His frame of reference is broad, drawing on poetry, literature and art, at times referring to natural and social sciences, delving into psychology, using metaphors and allusions, sharing his thoughts, full of wise observations of practical value.

This publication is a welcome, significant and timely event that will enrich any music library. It is doubly meaningful to those who knew and worked with Dr. Fierro at CSUN and beyond. Addressed to musicians, pianists and music lovers alike, these succinct, witty and probing essays promise to be truly appreciated by readers.

Dmitry Rachmanov, DMA
Professor, Chair of Keyboard Studies
California State University, Northridge

Introduction

Charles Fierro, one of California's leading pianists, toured as a concert artist for the National Endowment for the Arts and the California Arts Council and gave more than twenty-five concerto performances with orchestras. He appeared twice at the National Gallery of Art and the Dumbarton Oaks Foundation in Washington, D.C., and was selected to perform the American Bicentennial Recital at the Palace of Fontainebleau in France on the personal invitation of legendary musician, Nadia Boulanger. He was known for his interpretations of music by Beethoven, Schumann and Liszt at the Ojai Festivals and performed more than a dozen times at the prestigious Monday Evening Concerts in Los Angeles, presenting American premieres of important new works.

A recording artist, Charles debut for Nonesuch Records was named "Critics' Choice" for five consecutive months by *High Fidelity Magazine*. His recording of the piano music of Aaron Copland was made under the auspices of the composer himself. For Delos International, he recorded MacDowell's *Sonata Eroica* and *Twelve Virtuoso Etudes*. For Nonesuch, he recorded MacDowell's *Keltic Piano Sonata*, *Sea Pieces*, and *Woodland Sketches* and the world premiere recording of MacDowell's *First Modern Suite*.

For over thirty years, Charles was a Professor of Music at California State University, Northridge, where he received the Distinguished Teaching Award. He was known for his inspiring classes in all aspects of the piano repertory. A recognized educator, he lectured at the New England Conservatory in Boston, taught at the Image International Music Festival and served on the Board of Directors of the Paderewski Music Society. He was also the author of numerous published articles on musical subjects as well as chamber music reviews which have appeared in the international press.

Charles Fierro studied piano with Lillian Steuber, Adele Marcus and Joanna Graudan and musicology and conducting with composer Ingolf Dahl, whose major piano works he recorded on the Orion label. At the completion of his graduate studies, he was awarded a Doctorate of Music "with Distinction" from the University of Southern California. In his later years as Professor Emeritus of Piano at California State University, Northridge Charles remained active performing concerts, lecturing and adjudicating.

PART I
THOUGHTS ON MUSIC

Charles enjoyed sharing his thoughts on all things music. The articles that follow represent a wide array of subjects that were important to him and of value to musicians and aficionados alike.

Aaron Copland—An Easy Person to Know

A tall, friendly man, Aaron Copland was an easy person to know. Over lunch at the Brown Derby, he told me humorous stories about his student days in Paris and about his experiences as a Hollywood film composer.

My introduction to his piano music had happened when I was a music major in college. Listening to a broadcast of his *Piano Variations,* I was struck by the rightness of the music. It sounded exactly as I imagined modern music ought to sound. I purchased the score immediately and shocked my teacher by playing it at the next lesson.

Subsequently, association with composers Ingolf Dahl and Lawrence Morton, both close friends of Copland, increased my enthusiasm, so it was natural for me to play a recital of his music when he visited Los Angeles in 1975.

From this came the invitation from Nadia Boulanger to perform the program in Paris and the contract to record the music for Delos International.

By that time, Aaron and I had become friends. We corresponded frequently and I would send him programs and reviews. He took a lively interest in young musicians and was always encouraging them. This generosity of spirit set an example for professionals and amateurs alike and is one of the reasons so many musicians take pleasure remembering him.

Summer 2000

The Piano Music of Aaron Copland

So long as the human spirit thrives on this planet, music in some living form will accompany and sustain it and give it expressive meaning.

—Aaron Copland

Several times during his career, Aaron Copland turned to his "native" instrument, the piano, and enriched its literature with significant and substantial works. His keyboard catalogue includes, in addition to the titles discussed in this article, the *Piano Concerto* (1926), *Four Piano Blues* (published in 1949) and an assortment of shorter pieces for young players.

On the surface, Copland's piano music appears to be radically different from the folksy Americana by which he is best known. How could the lofty *Piano Fantasy* come from the same pen as *Billy the Kid*? A closer look behind their apparently contrary styles shows a single set of values at work: directness of expression, primacy of melody and rhythm, absolute clarity of form, even some of the same harmonies. Copland always proclaimed tonality. Even in his most dissonant music (the *Piano Variations*), one can readily identify chord roots, key centers and a conventional harmonic plan. At a fundamental level, Copland the "modernist" and Copland the "populist" are really one and the same.

Copland's endowments were apparent from the beginning. The *Passacaglia* (1922) reveals the young composer not only in command of his craft but with something important to say. Dedicated to Nadia Boulanger' to whom

Copland had entrusted his advanced training in Paris, the *Passacaglia* continues French neoclassical traditions in its serious intent, logical organization and omnipresent tonality. Its searching eight-measure bass theme reappears in counterpoint to chromatic lines, in arpeggiated figuration and in *ostinati*, with motivic elements emphasized for their structural value.

Copland's masterpiece, *Piano Variations*, was considered revolutionary when it appeared in 1930. By that time, Copland had his own ideas and he had developed a highly individual manner of expressing them. It was a style as virtuosic as Liszt's, but used to create a new sound-world of angular beauty—taut, dramatic, economical. Each variation, clearly delineated in character, explores the latent possibilities of the opening four-note motto and of the ten-measure theme as a whole. Harmonic confrontations and reiterative, irregular meters forge many diverse moods. At its climax the music enacts a life-death struggle between sound and silence.

The *Piano Sonata* (1941) rightly belongs among the finest examples of that form. Its message is universal; its tone is noble, its compositional craft subtle and consummately assured. Like a biblical prophet, Copland foresaw the devastation that would take place in his time; hence the elegiac character of the first movement. He uses the piano's sonorities to simulate great bells tolling in warning and lamentation, yet from this dark atmosphere a jazzy development emerges. It is remarkable how Copland takes seemingly incompatible ideas and integrates them at a high level. The second movement's tenuous lines, imitating Appalachian folk instruments, compulsively repeat a few elements over and over, creating a restless scherzo that changes from "delicate" to "crude" (composer's words). Amid the solemn chords that introduce the last movement, a lonely bugle call, echoing from far away like military "taps", deepens the feeling of loss and grief. An anthem appears, tentatively at first, then rises phrase by phrase to a grand peroration. At the strategic moment, Copland unifies the entire *Sonata* with a single master stroke by bringing back the opening theme from the first movement. The music subsides in a coda of peace and reconciliation.

The *Piano Fantasy* (1952-57) is a visionary work of extraordinary scope. The music ranges far and wide with seemingly inexhaustible imagination. Supporting this diversity of ideas is a monumental arch: slow-fast-slow, a plan favored by the composer. Declamatory single notes and clangorous fourth-chords announce the first and last parts. Between these landmarks are numerous contrasting subsections, developments, transitions and reminiscences. The concluding pages attain a sublime transcendence.

Night Thoughts, composed for the 1973 Van Cliburn Competition, challenges the interpreter's powers of introspection. Subtitled *Homage to Ives,* the music, whether tender or impassioned, remains lyrical throughout. Simple melodies, sensitively shaded textures and eloquent polytonal harmonies contribute to the evocative atmosphere of this short essay. The horn-call question with which it begins receives its expected answer only in the final measures.

Altogether, Aaron Copland's piano music is one of the proudest boasts of twentieth-century keyboard repertory. Its originality and technical perfection make it immediately identifiable. It addresses our lives with optimism and wisdom. Because it "rings true", I believe it will speak to the future as well.

Summer 2000

To listen to Charles' CD of **Copland: Piano Music** ***on Apple Music,*** ***see Links on page 121.***

Ingolf Dahl—A Personal Reminiscence

I first met Ingolf Dahl at a dice game. Actually, it was a chamber music concert celebrating the sixtieth birthday of the American composer, Aaron Copland, in November 1960. Many prominent musicians took part in the performance, including the composer-pianists Leo Smith, Lukas Foss and Dahl himself.

I clearly remember the occasion. The all-Copland program opened with the early piano trio, *Vitebsk* (1928), continued with the *Piano Fantasy* (1957), *Two Pieces* for string quartet (1928), the cantata *In the Beginning* (1947), and concluded with the exhilarating *Danzón Cubano* (1942) for two pianos. Dahl, Smith and Foss were all friends of Copland and had played both piano parts of the *Danzón* many times, but left it to chance to determine which two would perform the piece at the concert. So they rolled dice on stage! (The game was also a humorous comment on the emerging fashion for introducing "chance" into music.) Dahl and Foss "won" and played the piece with breathtaking precision and élan. A telegram from Copland arrived to express appreciation for the tribute.

Ingolf Dahl enjoyed a legendary reputation as a composer, conductor, pianist, musicologist and educator. Before meeting him, I envisaged a towering figure of overwhelming seriousness. You may imagine my surprise on encountering a stocky, balding, fun-loving individual with a robust build from hiking, mountain climbing and skiing!

Born in 1912 of Swedish parents in Hamburg, Germany, he received his musical education in Switzerland under the direction of Phillip Jarnach, a composer in the Busoni circle. As a young musician, Dahl conducted operas in Zurich. He emigrated to the United States in 1938, settling in Los Angeles where he worked at a popular radio station. Years later, he spoke proudly of his arrangement of the cowboy ballad "*Don't Fence Me In*". In 1945 he accepted a position at the University of Southern California as conductor of the orchestra and professor of musicology. He became a friend and close associate of Igor Stravinsky, who lived in Hollywood. Dahl enjoyed telling the story about the time he was about to carve the turkey at a Thanksgiving dinner when the phone rang. The great Russian composer had completed his *Symphony in Three Movements* that day and wanted Ingolf to play it with him at the piano. (Dahl was a phenomenal score-reader). Turkey and guests were abandoned as he drove off to Stravinsky's house for a first reading of the new masterpiece.

At USC Dahl taught a celebrated seminar on the music of Stravinsky. His engaging lectures covered the music of Stravinsky's Russian predecessors, the stylistic development of his sensational early ballet scores, the influential compositions of his neoclassical period and the adoption of serial techniques in his later music.

While taking this course, I was preparing Schoenberg's *Three Piano Pieces, op. 11*, for an upcoming recital. Late one evening Dahl asked me to play them for him. He listened attentively, making a few comments about taking time to project details. A few weeks later, a flu epidemic devastated the musical community in Los Angeles. Lawrence Morton, manager of the prestigious Monday Evening Concerts, telephoned Dahl to ask if there was anyone who could "fill in" at the last moment for an ailing artist. Dahl, always ready to help young musicians, recommended my name. On the night of the performance, the hall was filled to capacity. Mr. and Mrs. Stravinsky were there, along with music critics from several newspapers. My "debut" with the Schoenberg pieces went well and in the years that followed, I had the good fortune to play much contemporary music, especially by living composers.

One of these composers was Dahl himself. At that time, Professor John Crown was hosting a syndicated television series devoted to the history of piano music; he asked me to play Dahl's *Sonata Pastorale* (dedicated to Crown) on a program to be broadcast (at 6:00 a.m.!) a few weeks later.

Dahl did not own a TV set, so on the morning of the broadcast, he drove to Crown's house to watch the program, after which they celebrated with a champagne breakfast!

Another of Dahl's distinguished courses was a graduate seminar entitled Music of the Classic and Early Romantic Period. Here we studied the music of C. P. E. Bach, Gluck, Haydn, Mozart, Beethoven, Schubert and Rossini. We also learned about Graun, Pergolesi, Wagenseil, Reicha and Sammartini, composers whose names we scarcely remember today but who contributed significantly to the development of the classical style.

For me, however, the most memorable of Dahl's enterprises was his *Collegium Musicum*, a course devoted to the preparation and performance of early music. For three hours every Wednesday evening we gathered to sing, conduct and play everything from Gregorian chant to secular works of the French Baroque. We particularly enjoyed transcribing and editing motets by Machaut, Dufay and Dunstable and "realizing" canons by Palestrina, Lassus and many others. Afterwards, our group would meet at a local ice cream parlor where Dahl once remarked that a sure recipe for bliss was a mass by Obrecht and a root beer float!

Perhaps the greatest honor I received from Dahl was his request that I accompany a baritone in the first performance of his new *Cycle of Sonnets* on poems by Petrarch. Dahl set the medieval Italian text in an expressive modern style, complete with madrigalistic tone painting. Busy with the complicated piano part, I did not notice that at one spot, the baritone had misread a ledger line, singing F-sharp instead of D-sharp. When we reached that measure at the first rehearsal for Dahl, he pointed out the error, then said, "Actually, F-sharp sounds better!" "But how about the tone row?", we wondered. "There are plenty of D-sharps around," replied Dahl; "F-sharp sounds better." So we changed the note in the score.

Summer 2004

In memorium concert honoring Ingolf Dahl

Paying Forward

I am grateful to my late friend and colleague, Professor Stephen Eberhart, for introducing me to the ancient Egyptian practice of Ma'at. I write about it here because of its particular applicability to music study. But first a word about Steve.

I met him in December, 1993, a smallish man with a round face and round glasses, wearing a cherubic smile as he carried an enormous wreath across the university quadrangle. A holiday decoration? I had to inquire. It was, he explained, a prop to illustrate a concept for a class in Cultural History of Mathematics. He was writing a book on the subject and one of my piano students happened to be in his class.

As we became acquainted over the next few months, he conversed learnedly on every topic imaginable and, in fact, knew more about music than I did. He was a mathematician who had majored in bassoon at Oberlin Conservatory and music theory in Munich, Germany, completing there the training in Hindemith's *The Craft of Musical Composition*. He was vastly knowledgeable about performers, conductors and recordings. His favorite composers were as diverse as Haydn, Berlioz, Schoenberg and the Englishman Havergal Brian.

I especially remember his first letter to me. It was dated in Mayan glyphs! He was urging me to see the new production of *Swan Lake* in the radical scenario by the British choreographer, Matthew Bourne. I attended a performance of the ballet and phoned Steve to tell him about my enthusiasm. It turns out that he had seen it twenty-one times between Los Angeles, New York and London and had been a guest at a reception for the artists. I then learned that he was an expert in the music of Tchaikovsky. He sent me an analytical article about the music and gave me a new biography of the composer by the Russian scholar, Alexander Poznansky. It should not have surprised me that a person of such diverse interests would have knowledge about ancient Egyptian art and philosophy. Toward the end of his life he presented a lecture on the subject to a meeting of the Anthroposophical Society in Pasadena. A mutual friend, Jean Brousseau, was present and sent me a copy of Steve's lecture notes.

The basic idea of Ma'at is that of paying forward. When someone does something for us, we repay the favor not to the person who performed the favor, but to someone else, who will then do the same for someone else in the future. This seemed to be an apt description of the act of teaching, especially in music, where the relationships tend to be one-on-one.

In Egyptian lore, Ma'at was personified as a goddess with a feather in her hair. She was the overseer of benign human relations, interested in the continuation of culture in the broad sense. I like to think that the feather was not a mere adornment but a talisman, a visible reminder to her devotees to practice the consciousness that she herself symbolized.

Steve put it this way, "As a concept underlying social life, Ma'at was expressed in cultivating memory of good deeds and extending them forward, thus remembering those of an earlier generation and being remembered by those of the next."

Nowadays, information of all kinds is available everywhere. If education involved only the transmission of data, we would not need teachers. But we do need teachers, not merely to analyze, guide and inspire, but to provide a relational context for learning. In a real sense, student and teacher learn together; hence the phrase "to study with someone".

I once heard an academic administrator state publicly that college is a "business", education is a "product" and students are "customers". This debased view strikes me as materialistic, shortsighted and cynical, utterly failing to understand the functional reality of the learning experience. Teaching is more than a job, it is a relationship. Its value to society is beyond price. Ma'at reminds us of the "debt" incurred in receiving instruction by encouraging us to contribute to the advancement of culture in the next generation. In doing so, we are not merely repeating what we learned from our teachers who were repeating what they learned from their teachers; we are adding something original and personal. This is the genuine tradition.

The practice of mindfulness also counteracts our all-too-human inclination to take things for granted. Our early ancestors knew perfectly well that the sun rises every morning and the days begin to lengthen at the winter solstice, yet they performed ritual chants and dances, not to make these phenomena happen, but to remind themselves not to take them for granted. Similarly, the abundant amenities we enjoy in modern life do not appear automatically or by chance, but through the efforts of untold numbers of individuals. We do well not to take these for granted either.

The wisdom imparted to us by educators is certainly one of these amenities; as such, it is both an inheritance and a responsibility. By remembering our teachers and paying forward to our students, we create solidarity with the past and the future; we see our work in long-term perspective and understand our role, however small, in music history.

Spring 2005

Has MacDowell's Time Come Again?

For one who has lived with the music of Edward MacDowell for twenty five years, it is tempting to write of him as though he were in the pantheon of established composers. This is particularly so when we realize that during his lifetime (1860-1908), even in his middle thirties, he was widely regarded as "the great American composer". One critic even esteemed his piano sonatas as "by far the best since

Beethoven". Virtually everything he wrote was published and his music appeared in the repertoires of international artists. As a pianist, he was compared to Paderewski when he performed his concertos with major orchestras in the United States and Europe. Moreover, he served as Professor of Music at Columbia University in New York, authored *Critical and Historical Essays* (a compilation of his university lectures) and was the subject of countless magazine articles.

MacDowell's compositional career spanned barely two decades (1881-1901). During those years, a multitude of responsibilities left him little time to compose, yet his output comprises over sixty works, including two orchestral suites, four symphonic poems, numerous songs and works for vocal ensemble. For the piano there are two concertos, four large sonatas, two suites and eighteen collections of tone poems, some, like the *Twelve Virtuoso Etudes*, quite substantial. To remember MacDowell solely as the composer of *To a Wild Rose* is as unfair as remembering Beethoven solely for *Für Elise* or Brahms only for his *Lullaby*. (Nineteenth century composers relied heavily for their living on royalties from the sales of sheet music. The sheer quantity of short pieces and picturesque titles may say more about society and the publishing business than about aesthetic values.)

Although MacDowell utilized Native American themes for one of his major works, the *Indian Suite* for orchestra, he was most definitely not a nationalistic composer. He had sharp criticism for what he regarded as Dvorak's facile adoption of American folk material. In his later years, he even refused to allow his music to be performed on all-American programs. He thought of himself as an internationalist and wanted his works to stand comparison with the best European music.

A hiker and photographer, MacDowell responded sensitively to nature, the land and the sea in all their colors and moods.

His piano pieces, *From a Wandering Iceberg* and *In Deep Woods* are splendid examples. Like Schumann, he was enormously well read and always found inspiration in literature; naturally, his music has a programmatic bearing. Mottos from Carolingian romance, Arthurian legend and Nordic sagas appear among his titles, along with quotations from major British, German and American poets, yet he insisted that his music be understood as a commentary on the narrative or pictorial content, rather than as a description of it.

The roots of his style are firmly planted in the traditions of Mendelssohn, Schumann and Liszt; melody and character are paramount. Some aspects of his later music, however, strike us as forward-looking and at least as modern as early Debussy. Highly effective writing for the piano in both his dramatic and mystical works includes layered sonorities, pedal effects and a very personal use of harmony which makes his music immediately identifiable. Several of his most famous collections, such as the *Woodland Sketches*, *Sea Pieces*, *Fireside Tales* and *New England Idylls* contain pieces for intermediate level pianists.

When Western music took a radical shift of direction in the early twentieth century, Romantic ideals were suddenly devalued, so it is not surprising that much nineteenth century music, including MacDowell's, was placed "on hold" to await rediscovery at a later time. In the 1940s, MacDowell's widow, Marian, predicted that his time would come again. Today, the re-awakening of interest in nineteenth century music and the renewal of Romantic values in contemporary music provide a perfect opportunity to test the validity of her foresight. Indeed, the music of his contemporaries, Mahler and Elgar, has enjoyed significant revival in recent years. MacDowell's rightful place in music history is up to the judgment of the listening public, of course, but this judgment cannot be made unless the music is played.

Winter 2002

The King Arthur Sonata

Edward MacDowell's *Sonata Eroica* (1895) is a masterful example of Romantic program music: it depicts characters and tells a story. The composer did not supply a detailed program for the piece, but on the title page he inscribed, "Arthur Flower of Kings", leaving no doubt that the music is "about" the famous British monarch and the Knights of the Round Table.

The *Sonata* opens with a portrait of the king himself, noble, grave, valiant. The mood soon becomes restless, reflecting Arthur's tumultuous reign. Next, a beautiful Celtic melody describes Queen Guinevere and Arthur's loyalty to his people. A spirited closing theme seems to foretell Arthur's triumph over his enemies. This leads to a dramatic development section that presents these ideas in a new light.

The second movement is a mysterious scherzo that suggests the king's magical connection with spirits of the forest. Minor keys and modal scales evoke the atmosphere of a country where skies are often cloudy.

The third movement is a grand adagio depicting the passionate love affair between Queen Guinevere and Sir Lancelot, Arthur's most trusted knight. These two betray their king and conspire to ally themselves with Arthur's traitorous nephew, Sir Mordred.

The final movement vividly describes the furious clash of Mordred's forces against the armies of the king. At the height of battle, Arthur is mortally wounded. The music portrays his final agony and a chilling silence signals the moment of his death on the battlefield. The story and the sonata are not tragic, however. The radiant coda symbolizes King Arthur's glorification in history and legend.

The *Sonata Eroica* is a kind of symphony for solo piano. Not the least of the demands it makes on the pianist is the need to maintain a "long line" amid extremely contrasting events. (In the first movement alone there are twelve metronomic tempo markings!) The writing is almost orchestral, with a dynamic range from quadruple *piano* to quadruple *forte*. The harmonic palette includes chords of the seventh, ninth and thirteenth, typical for the period.

MacDowell fuses classical sonata form with cyclical technique. Leitmotifs and individual themes retain their identity even as they undergo constant change. The fact that these ideas also combine contrapuntally shows that MacDowell planned the entire work in advance. Because of these unifying devices and the overall conception of the piece, the sonata makes sense in both musical and narrative terms.

Fall 2014

To purchase recordings of Charles Fierro performing MacDowell's music, see Links on page 122.

A Giant of 20th Century Music—Paul Hindemith

When he first appeared on the European musical scene in the 1920s, Paul Hindemith amazed listeners with the kinetic energy and freewheeling dissonances of his compositions. An anti-Romantic attitude gave his music a clever "expressionist" edge. In his ironic *Suite 1922*, he treats the piano like a machine, applying "abrasive arrogance"

(Glenn Gould's characterization) to popular dance forms like the Shimmy, Boston and Ragtime. His brilliant, iconoclastic *Kammermusik* series for diverse ensembles toppled traditional notions of beauty. At the same time, he produced the affecting song cycle, *Das Marienleben* and the witty *Wind Quintet*.

In the early 1930s, however, Hindemith's style underwent a sea change. As he himself said, "Music, despite its tendency toward abstraction, is basically a means of communication", consequently, "composers and performers have a social responsibility to be comprehensible."

At that critical time, the prevailing feeling was that standard harmonic practice had been depleted; composers were searching for new source materials. Hindemith, instead, single-handedly undertook the renewal of the entire tonal system.

To accomplish this, he placed the art of music on a foundation of natural principles, in particular, the overtone series and the psycho-acoustic facts of sound perception. In his groundbreaking book, *The Craft of Musical Composition*, he proposed that the materials of music are not only the diatonic scale and its chromatic alterations, but that all twelve notes of an octave can legitimately be derived from a fundamental tone and are therefore related to it. "Tonality", he declared, "is a natural force, like gravity. It cannot be suspended for long without engendering confusion in the listener."

In his theory and in his music, Hindemith found a way to utilize the full spectrum of "chromatic" resource while retaining conventional notions of tension and release, dissonance and resolution. Above all, he affirmed the primacy of the major triad as a symbol and expression of order. He consciously chose related key areas for subsidiary themes and structural relationships. This organization gives his music perspective, a third dimension like that in representational painting.

Of course, adherence to a system, no matter how comprehensive and natural, does not guarantee results, nor does technical know-how substitute for ideas. Hindemith was, in fact, a fountain of ideas. Like Mozart, he composed quickly, yet his music is perfectly crafted in every detail and shows no sign of haste. He believed that music has the ethical power to affect human character and that listeners have the ability to use their musical experiences for the betterment of the world. He organized sound successions to reflect the harmony of mind and body, the beauty of mathematical proportions and even the laws that govern the cosmos. His music abounds with a feeling of health and optimism. Without sermonizing, it tends toward no less a goal than the moral improvement of humanity by attempting to align the human spirit with the harmony of the heavens.

Even if he had not composed a note, Hindemith would be one of the giants of twentieth-century music. His contributions to the theory and philosophy of music have universal validity but it is the power of his compositions themselves that continues to reach us emotionally. "Neo-Baroque", "Neoclassical" and other reductionist labels do not do justice to the striking individuality and significance of his work.

One reason for the comprehensibility of his music is its clear relationship to tradition, especially the counterpoint of J. S. Bach, Beethoven's technique of motivic derivation, the pianistic textures of Brahms, Schumann's chains of dotted rhythms, the modal cadences and open fourths and fifths of early Renaissance style. Yet his music is personal and non-eclectic. For all its modernity, it speaks a language we can understand. Hindemith's style is immediately identifiable. His music sounds like nobody else's.

We relate to his music because of its moods and forms (cheerful, solemn, energetic, pastorale, march, etc.) are familiar from our life experience and because even his most complicated pieces retain an essential vocal connection. In his book, *A Composer's World* (which I highly recommend), he writes: "Whatever a pianist does, using intellect, hands and lever arrangements in the process of enlivening musical forms, will always be derived from musical experiences with the human voice. If pianists want to move listeners intellectually and emotionally, they would better stay close to the conditions of vocal expression. Even in *prestissimo* tone successions, so easily produced by faultlessly working keyboards, the reference to the basic musical material of the singing voice should always be recognizable."

Throughout his professional life, Hindemith was committed to education. He taught at a number of institutions of higher learning, including Yale University. During my apprenticeship, I had hoped to study conducting, musicology, performance practice, composition, analysis—anything—with him. By the time I was ready to do so, he had retired and moved to Switzerland where he died in 1963. However, the legacy of his music and ideas remains. Like other composers of prodigious creativity, his output is uneven but his best works, like the *Sinfonia Serena* and *Nobilissima Visione*, attain a high degree of inspiration. His output for the piano is comparatively small but significant. My plans for the near future include performances of the three *Piano Sonatas, The Four Temperaments,* the complete *Ludus Tonalis* and a number of chamber music pieces and, if I can find the right soprano, the *Marienleben* cycle.

Except for the perennial popularity of orchestral works like the *Symphony Mathis der Maler* and the *Symphonic Metamorphoses on Themes of Carl Maria von Weber*, Hindemith's music was eclipsed by the avant-garde of the 1950s and '60s. Melody, continuity, metric rhythm and tonality fell out of fashion. Even the notion of what music is came into question. All this led to a "barbarous" (Hindemith's word) musical culture without a common language; in effect, a virtual Tower of Babel.

More recently, we see a trend toward mere entertainment in some concert music. Colorful effects, superficial simplification and easy accessibility show more concern about the box office than about enduring values. In this context, the depth and integrity of Hindemith's music is more relevant than ever. Yes, he believed in communication, but he also believed that there must be something important to communicate. As he said in one of his lectures: "The inexhaustibility of artistic forms is the inexhaustibility of human thought itself. If a musician has the gift of showing, with the means of expression related to his times and circumstances, a reflection of this inexhaustibility to his fellow men and bringing into existence, together with them and on their behalf, a small universe, then he has fulfilled his artistic task."

Summer 2008

A Rainbow in Music

Since the sixteenth century, composers have reserved some of their music for special audiences who appreciate subtleties of technique and meaning. Occasionally works like these carry modest designations. Bach, for example, called his *Goldberg Variations* "exercises", yet everyone would agree that this is one of his most sublime creations.

Paul Hindemith's *Ludus Tonalis* belongs to this type of music. The composer calls it "studies in counterpoint, tonal organization and piano playing", and like the *Goldberg Variations*, it is far more than an academic exercise. It is his largest work for solo piano, a contrapuntal tour de force and a masterpiece of art and philosophy.

Free from the need to provide mere entertainment, Hindemith provides the pianist and the audience with music of far-reaching consequence. There are no sensational effects, no virtuosic displays, only pure music. The twenty-five pieces in this famous work are "etudes" in the sense that they present technical challenges while at the same time remaining joyful, even light-hearted. *Ludus Tonalis,* after all, means "A Play of Notes" or "A Game of Tonalities".

The title itself is a kind of manifesto. *Ludus Tonalis* demonstrates in actual music that expanded tonality is an inexhaustible resource for composition and, indeed, necessary for music to make sense. Hindemith's harmonic style is a synthesis of tonality and chromaticism: key centers govern the overall design; melodies and chords have identifiable roots; there are characteristic cadences, pedal points, sequential writing and, above all, a feeling of tension and repose.

Ludus Tonalis has an outward similarity to Bach's *Well-Tempered Clavier*. However, the work is not really a collection but an integral unity and Hindemith means it to be played that way. Its individual pieces are like the colors of a rainbow, radiant and distinct, leading from one to the next. In fact, the whole work is like a great arc, reaching its climax in the seventh interlude, marked "very broad".

Ludus Tonalis begins and ends in the key of C. Each of the twelve fugues is in a different key and each interlude anticipates the following fugue by key and motivic relationships. Also, each fugue is of a different kind, written with magisterial skill and authority. Despite sophisticated compositional techniques, the content of the fugues is always about mood. One can readily imagine scenarios for any of them.

The interludes are character pieces in the tradition of Schumann, Debussy and others. Here you will find songs, dances, scene painting, a march, a toccata, etc. These "fleeting visions" add to the listener's pleasure by alluding to Western music from medieval to modern times.

The prelude and postlude are three-part fantasies in the Baroque manner and are reversed inversions of each other. The prelude begins with enthusiasm and expectancy; the postlude ends in celestial wisdom and peace.

All of Hindemith's creative output is meant to symbolize and express the order of the universe and to promote the ethical benefit of humanity. This ancient concept of the moral purpose of music is accomplished when the listener imaginatively and empathetically participates in the experience.

Summer 2012

To watch Charles perform* Ludus Tonalis *at CSUN in 2012 on YouTube, see Links page 121.

The Piano Sonatas of Paul Hindemith

Piano Sonata No. 1

Paul Hindemith spent the winter of 1935-36 in Ankara, Turkey, on a commission to organize the music education system in that country. While there, he planned the cycle of the three *Piano Sonatas,* completing the project upon his return to the Continent. It was a time of ominous political developments in Europe. Officials of the Third Reich had recently banned public performances of his music in Germany.

Hindemith rarely spoke about his own music, but in a prefatory note, he credits "*Der Main*", a poem by the nineteenth-century German poet, Friedrich Holderlin, for providing the inspiration for the first *Piano Sonata*. Professor John Irving of the CSUN Language Department, made an elegant translation for me. In it, the poet dreams about an idealized ancient Greece, a land once ringing with songs and dances of a happy, highly civilized people on the shores of the blue Aegean, but now in ruins, devastated by wars and oppression. Evidently, Hindemith saw a parallel to what was happening in his own country. Though the connection of the music to the poem is of a general nature only, the *Sonata* is very much a product of its moment in history.

The music is symphonic in dimensions and presents an extraordinary range of moods. As in Beethoven, the opening phrase of the first movement generates the principal themes of the entire work. This technique creates subconscious cross-references throughout the piece while allowing maximum freedom to the composer's imagination.

The overall design of the work is unusual: none of the movements is in sonata form. The first and fourth movements are variants of one another. The first and second movements go together; the fourth and fifth go together. The third stands by itself. The *Sonata* opens thoughtfully with two melodies, the first in bright A major, the second in dark E minor. Elaboration begins right away, with no hint of the later significance of these themes.

The solemn processional in the second movement is one of the noblest in the piano repertory. The grief here is real; there are tears in the ink for the loss of thousands in the First World War. The music attempts to transcend the grief, builds to a great climax, then ends with resignation in one of the most sublime passages in twentieth-century music.

The extraverted third movement has all the pseudo-excitement of a (Nazi?) parade (ironically in triple metre!). While the sonorities blare, the composer daydreams; memories of tender old songs (and better times) float in and out. The prominent sound of chimes and the rude parade music try to bring him back to "reality". The resulting sadness that naturally follows is magically lifted during the silence between the two themes of the next movement. From here on, the *Sonata* takes a positive direction. The finale bursts in with a boisterous gigue and a humorous transition. An important cadence leads to a jolly dance tune. In the movement's central section, however, a fanfare introduces a serious idea in the lower registers of the piano. After a brief development, the gigue returns, builds to a grandiose climax and ends with a festive coda. I am indebted to pianist Jon Sakata for the observation that in Hindemith's music, every movement is like a panel in a tryptich where the intense identification of time the cumulative energy of the whole is greater than the sum of its parts.

Piano Sonata No. 2

If the first *Sonata* is orchestral in concept, the second *Sonata* is more like chamber music. It opens with a graceful allegro, followed by a lighthearted, slightly delirious waltz. The emotional depth of the third movement elegy lends weight and significance to the *Sonata*. A cheerful rondo follows immediately. It appears to be unrelated at first, but gradually reveals itself to be a variant of the elegy. The chorale that concludes both the elegy and the rondo invokes a benediction.

Piano Sonata No. 3

In this, his most popular keyboard work, Hindemith summons all the resources of the piano and the pianist. It is a tour de force of melodic inventiveness and contrapuntal wizardry. The lilting melodies of the opening movement are reminiscent of English folksongs. As they grow, they accumulate waves of sound, then gradually vanish. Sensitive passages in parallel harmonies lend an impressionistic touch rare in Hindemith.

In total contrast, the second movement interrupts with a compulsive scherzo and a fleet-fingered trio. There is no slow movement. Instead, Hindemith writes a movement whose determined tread and tenor range remind us of a labor union march (possibly suggesting the composer's proletarian sympathies). Its middle and concluding sections, in the "*piccolo*" register of the piano, offer a vision of hope. In between, there appears a shadowy *fugato* that is later integrated into the final movement. The *Sonata*, and indeed, the cycle of the three *Sonatas*, culminates with a magnificent triple fugue.

Postscript

Almost all the major keyboard composers have been pianists who wrote for their own performances. Hindemith was a notable exception. For several years, he was the violist in the distinguished Amar String Quartet, but he could play all the orchestral instruments and reportedly never composed anything he could not perform himself.

He intuitively understood the piano and the natural movement of the hands. His writing sounds particularly rich because it is built on the resonant intervals of the overtone series. His scores are clearly marked with dynamics and phrasing, but he trusts the performer to determine pedaling and fingering. Even in virtuoso passages, he never indulges in empty display, preferring always to subordinate ego to content.

But these are details. The larger case I urge is that Hindemith belongs in the pantheon of twentieth-century composers and that his art is important to us today, inside and outside the concert hall. The proof is in the music.

Summer 2009

The "Last" Romantic Piano Piece—Arnold Schoenberg

Of the many musical compositions that lay claim to being the "last" Romantic work, Arnold Schoenberg's *Three Piano Pieces, op. 11,* presents a strong case. Like the Brahms' *Intermezzi* and *Capriccio,* these pieces are moody, probing, restless, defiant. They arise from subconscious dreams and fantasies about the loneliness and the anxiety of human experience. As such they represent the dark side of Romanticism.

Equally characteristic of their particular kind of Romanticism are the regret and nostalgia they evoke. No one knew the great tradition of European classical music better than Schoenberg. Imagine what courage it took to overturn centuries of the tradition he loved and to launch almost alone onto the uncharted seas of atonality!

The music is expressive and beautiful, but not meant to be "entertaining" in the ordinary sense of the word. This is not to say that the music is unemotional. Quite the contrary, it is intensely emotional, and the harmonic idiom is ideally suited to convey the inner substance of the music. With constantly fluctuating tempos, these pieces almost give the impression of improvisation, but they are in fact the product of careful planning. This is because Schoenberg, throughout his career, was very much concerned with structural unity and the derivation of an entire work from its opening ideas.

The pieces of *Opus 11* date from 1908, so their broader context is the critical period before the First World War. Revolutionary theories in sciences and the arts (Freud, Einstein, Darwin, James Joyce, Bertrand Russell) were in the air. Innovations by Debussy and Scriabin were undermining standard harmonic practice.

Schoenberg was a sensitive exponent of that age and one of the most influential thinkers in twentieth-century music. His ideas have affected almost every style of composition since then, yet his works are seldom performed today. As the late pianist Paul Jacobs has observed, the discussion about Schoenberg continues to bypass his music. This may be because, even after a century, some listeners find his music challenging, while conductors and soloists who are concerned about the box office tend to program other repertoire. Conversely, avant-garde composers of the 1950s and '60s long ago rejected his music as outdated.

This is why, for new listeners, it is useful to begin with his early music. Stylistically, *Opus 11* is transitional. Here we find plenty of familiar techniques alongside original ways of presenting them. Clear phrasing, thematic development, cadential figures, octave doubling, a feeling of tension and release, all of these continue standard practice, even while the music itself moves into a new esthetic territory.

It is also important to remember that the bulk of Schoenberg's early works are for the voice. Songs, cantatas and monodramas appear again and again in his catalog. There is even an extended aria for soprano in his *Second String Quartet*. So it is not surprising that these early piano pieces, at least the first two, are mostly melodic. If they were songs and had texts, those texts would surely be personal, even autobiographical, like several of the self-portraits he painted at that time. The third piece of *Opus 11*, however, is poles apart from the first two. Here Schoenberg is hurling thunderbolts of sound, contravening even his own principles of unity and form. There is very little that holds this piece together. Drastic confrontations of every kind undermine any sense of stability, yet among these violent outbursts are moments of utter sentimentality. Amazingly, these latter gestures (modified, of course) recall the operettas of Franz Lehar that were so popular in Vienna at the time. (Nostalgia, again!)

As we become familiar with this style, let's remember that this music is not an experiment. It is a fully realized masterpiece whose technical finesse and integrity of expression place it clearly in the line of character pieces by the great Romantics, especially Schumann. The content may be different, but the intent is the same.

Fall 2013

Guillaume Lekeu

It is exciting to introduce to our audiences a composer highly admired in Europe and other parts of the world. His music speaks directly and movingly to the hearts of music lovers and we are privileged to have important masterpieces from his pen.

Guillaume Lekeu was Belgian by birth, but considered himself French, since he lived most of his life in France. His dates (1870-1894) mark him as a contemporary of Scriabin, Ravel, Rachmaninoff, Schoenberg and novelist Marcel Proust. As a youth he learned violin and piano and eagerly studied musical scores. At fifteen he was introduced to the string quartets of Beethoven, an experience that changed his life: he decided to become a composer.

Until the age of twenty, without instruction in composition, he wrote a great deal of music, including ambitious works for symphony orchestra and chamber ensembles. These works, like the *String Quartets, Sonata for Cello and Piano* and *Trio for Violin, Cello and Piano* are apprentice projects, yet they contain many passages that forecast his later music. It is after studying counterpoint with César Franck in 1890 that he achieved artistic maturity.

His *Adagio for String Orchestra,* written in the spring of 1891, is a work of astonishing emotional depth and technical perfection. It is a magnificent elegy in memory of Franck, who had died a few months earlier. In July 1891 he entered the Prix de Rome Competition with the dramatic cantata *Andromède for Four Vocal Soloists, Chorus and Orchestra.* The following year the renowned violinist Eugène Ysaÿe commissioned him to write a *Sonata for Piano and Violin,* a magnificent piece that Ysaÿe played everywhere and which is now standard in the repertory.

Lekeu was an inspired melodist and an eloquent exponent of Late Romanticism. His musical ideas have immediate impact and enduring beauty. His harmonic language is rich, personal and readily identifiable. He admired Beethoven, Wagner and César Franck above all, yet his music is not at all like theirs.

One of the most original aspects of his music is his sophisticated use of cyclical form. He constructed memorable themes to sound in counterpoint with one another throughout an entire work. It goes without saying that this approach requires enormous contrapuntal skill and advanced planning.

We are fortunate to have more than 200 of his letters, edited and published in 1994 by Luc Verdebout. Writing in vivid French, he reveals a proud personality, enthusiastic about arts, philosophy and contemporary literature. His musical connections were with the avant-garde. He had strong opinions about the music of his time, criticizing composers who wrote frivolous entertainment and who had strayed from the noble purpose of music.

Several biographies of Lekeu have appeared, the most recent by Gilles Thiéblot in 2006. Lekeu's music is the subject of numerous dissertations, scholarly articles and websites. One of the earliest Lekeu enthusiasts was Claude Debussy, who played the piano part in an early performance of the *Quartet for Piano, Violin, Viola and Cello.* In 1923 the eminent musicologist and Librarian of Congress, Oscar Sonneck, declared that Lekeu's music does not suffer when played next to that of Beethoven. There are several commercial recordings of Lekeu's major works. His best known piece, the *Violin Sonata*, is particularly well represented on discs. The symphonic *Fantasy on Two Angevine Folk Songs,* which he himself conducted at its premiere, remains one of his most engaging and touching creations.

Was Lekeu an Impressionist? Certainly he would have been keenly interested in Debussy's iconic *Prelude to the Afternoon of a Faun,* but did not live to hear the first performance. However, his aesthetic orientation was always toward the expression of inner experience, rather than toward an impressionistic description of things. This is why he aligned with the Symbolist poets Paul Verlaine and Stéphane Mallarmé and the artist Carlos Schwabe. Lekeu himself was a poet of considerable gifts, as can be seen from the text of his *Trois Poèmes for Voice and Piano.* In a few deft lines he evokes tender melancholy, flirtatious humor and celestial ecstasy.

Of course, we cannot know how he might have developed as a composer over time. My guess is that he would have forged an independent style in modern music. Each of his works is highly individual; he intended that each should represent a stylistic and technical advance over its predecessors. No greater contrast could be imagined than between the radiance of the *Violin Sonata* and the dark passion of the (unfinished) *Piano Quartet*. In his mind Lekeu had worked out the themes for the third movement and was planning several large works when typhoid fever cut his life short at age twenty-four. I am not alone in believing that if he had had a normal lifespan, he would certainly have become one of the major figures of twentieth-century music. As we approach the 150th anniversary of his birth, we celebrate the masterworks he created. These are not only extremely beautiful and moving, but also important for our understanding of late nineteenth-century music. It is my intention to bring them to public performance in upcoming seasons.

Winter 2017

Classics

To reconstruct is to collaborate with time gone by,
Penetrating or modifying its spirit,And carrying it
toward a longer future.

—Marguerite Yourcenar

We classical musicians dedicate our lifetime to playing works from the past. Practitioners of the allied arts may find this anomalous, but to us it seems completely natural. In these historical artifacts, we find inspiration and emotional validation. These factors transcend time and style; our capacity to relate to them confirms the fundamental identity and continuum of human nature. The affective power of music results from the interaction of many forces, most of all from its identifiable character: we want music to "mean" something recognizable from our life experience. When this meaning appears, we "understand" the music.

In classical works, character is often conveyed in melodic line, whether overt or implied in figuration. The melodic principle engages our primary attention and touches us emotionally. As it binds together the various parts of a piece, it gives us something to hang onto: you can actually hum your way through a sonata or symphony. This partly accounts for the enduring appeal of great music and explains why works that fall short in melodic values also fall short in rousing a wider public.

In any of the arts, we need ideas to be put together in a convincing way. The Irish poet, Seamus Heaney, eloquently characterizes this interface between form and content. In the preface to his translation of the Anglo-Saxon epic *Beowulf*, he describes it as "a work of the greatest imaginative vitality, a masterpiece where the structuring of the tale is as elaborate as the beautiful contrivances of its language … Its narrative elements may belong to a previous age, but as a work of art it lives in its own continuous present, equal to our knowledge of reality in the present time. We claim it as an inheritance, upright, rudimentary, unshiftably planked in the long ago, yet willable forward again and again and again."

Organization of artistic ideas on a large scale necessarily entails complexity, sometimes to a very challenging degree. This is what keeps us fascinated by great music. Too much complexity, however, causes confusion; too little complexity generates predictability, as in a great deal of commercial popular music. The philosopher, Arthur Schopenhauer, observed that the finest compositions are the most difficult to understand. "They are only for the trained intelligence", he says. "They consist of long movements, where it is only after a labyrinthine maze that the fundamental note is recovered." He is referring, of course, to the Western tonal system.

The eminent theorist, Heinrich Schenker, demonstrates that the structural elaboration of large-scale works derives from this natural psycho-acoustical system with its cycle of fifths, related minors, modulatory possibilities, enharmonic equivalents, cadential drives, etc. Certainly this is true of music from the standard practice period, about 1700 to 1900. (Without assigning cause and effect, the sociologist Max Weber went so far as to propose that the development of the diatonic system corresponds to "rationalization" of the economy, namely capitalism!)

Composers of the eighteenth century wrote pieces for a specific occasion or for use during a particular season. They would have been astonished to find their works played hundreds of years later. Their way of thinking resembled that of modern filmmakers who expect their productions to "live" for a few weeks on screen then vanish into history. If we performers today had the same idea, we would play contemporary music exclusively and only for a current concert or tour, rarely reviving works from earlier seasons.

Our classic repertory is truly the inheritance of a long and noble past. "We stand on the shoulders of giants," (in Isaac Newton's felicitous phrase). Art music is not easy. It requires years of study, countless hours of immediate preparation and a great deal of courage in performance. Rather than acting as a deterrent, this "toughness" appeals to growth-minded individuals who want to reach for higher knowledge by re-creating great art and "carrying it to a longer future". When we bring this music to the public, we fulfill a social function and even an ethical purpose, especially if we believe, as the ancient philosophers did, that music is not merely entertainment, but that it contributes effectively to the moral improvement of its listeners. What better purpose could we find for our life's work?

Winter 2007

Listen to Your Teacher

"I want to play only the great works", she declared with a confident smile, "and I will start with the Tchaikovsky concerto". "What other concertos have you played?", I asked the prospective student. She hadn't played any, so I suggested that we might consider something else. "The *Emperor Concerto*!", she offered without hesitation. "Yes", I replied, "when you are ready!" Her expression changed and it became clear that I would not be able to work with her. I recommended that she go to another music school.

Quite apart from our discussion about repertory, it seems that this student's problem was a misunderstanding of the nature of a pedagogical relationship. Obviously, she had grown up in a market culture where the customer is always right and a business succeeds by giving consumers exactly what they want. We see this in the medical office, where patients demand a prescription for some drug they heard about on television, whether or not it fills their actual needs. Fundamentally, it comes down to a matter of trust. In an ideal learning situation, the teacher is the expert and the student follows the recommended repertory precisely. In some countries, the curriculum for performance majors in music schools is predetermined. For example, all freshmen study the same list of pieces before being promoted to the next level. I prefer the approach where the course of study is tailored to the needs of each student.

Teachers spend a lot of time behind the scenes selecting the right repertory for their students, pieces suited to the personality, technical advancement and musical understanding of each individual. Sometimes students offer valuable ideas about repertory and teachers certainly welcome this. More often, however, they want to take on music far beyond their present capacities, or they want to avoid certain composers or even entire style periods. Certainly, a teacher wants to use the student's enthusiasm for a certain piece as an incentive for study, but sometimes it is necessary to approach the situation diplomatically or negotiate a choice. "I'll let you play X if you will also play Y."

I believe in challenges but I do not believe in quantum leaps. For me, as a performer and teacher, a gradual, step-by-step approach works best , no shortcuts. Of course, no actual harm is done if we play a piece badly but how much real pleasure can we derive from playing something we love in a mediocre way? Would it not be more satisfying to give a superb performance of a less difficult piece?

Loving music and playing it well are different things. Much of what we call performance anxiety is really a reaction to a subconscious perception that the music in question is too difficult to handle under pressure. I believe we have to earn the right to play the advanced literature. This requires mature patience and a willingness to defer to the teacher's judgment.

Students and their parents sometimes assume that the purpose of music study is to win competitions and that certain pieces or certain types of pieces will virtually guarantee that result. As a consultant, I have worked with youngsters who had no business playing required competition pieces. Their whole effort was more about ego than art. In such cases, the worst thing that happens is that they win the competition, confirming them in their beliefs. In the end, it is the music that suffers.

One of the occupational hazards of our profession is that it tempts some people to fantasies of grandeur. However, no career can be based on illusions. A certain modesty and constant search for truth characterizes the best musicians I have known.

I feel proud of my former students who have gone on to become artists and teachers. Their success, I am quite certain, results from placing priority on music rather than on themselves. They serve society creatively, intelligently and with integrity. I am also proud of former students who have entered other professions while maintaining lively interest in music and the piano. They continue to grow and to support the arts in many essential ways.

All this starts with a proper relationship to our teachers. By following wholeheartedly their plan of instruction, by listening to what they say instead of dictating our own preferences, we will avoid needless disappointment and save a lot of time, and we may actually learn more about music and about ourselves.

Winter 2005

What Will You Play?

One of the most valuable things we do as musicians in society is to play for people. The piano recital, in particular, brings inspiration into a world which needs to be uplifted. This is why our potential listeners must be our first consideration when planning a program. Whom do we want to reach? What is their likely level of sophistication?

Once we have identified our target audience, the program we design becomes the single most important factor that will draw people to the recital hall, unless we are so famous that our name alone motivates them to hire a baby sitter, battle the freeways, search for parking, purchase tickets and sit through a performance on an evening when they would rather be watching TV!

But the music we select is important for another reason: what we play says as much about us as how we play it. The music we choose ideally represents us and our values. This is why the program as a whole should make sense; it should have an overall shape. Each piece should have a reason for being there; the program should not be merely an assortment of pieces we happen to be working on.

We pianists are heirs to the largest body of repertory in Western music, second only to that for voice. There is little excuse for playing only the most familiar or popular works, unless of course, we bring to them such original insights that they will seem like a revelation to listeners. My teacher, Ingolf Dahl, used to say that we ought to declare a twenty-five year moratorium on the standard repertory! By giving these works a good long "vacation", we could return to them with fresh ears and an open mind. We could experience the surprise and shock they conveyed when they were new.

The "well balanced" program resembling a menu, with representative examples from each style period, has proved durable because it is psychologically satisfying and capable of infinite variations. But there are other ways to go. A recital with a specific focus (a single composer, style period or form) can be effective if there is sufficient variety. A program I heard recently, devoted mostly to Russian salon music, succeeded because of the charm of the individual pieces and the commitment of the player. The late Jorge Bolet once played a recital of ballades (Grieg, Liszt, Chopin). On paper, this appeared risky, but the actual performance was engaging from beginning to end.

Winter, 2003

Interview Fall 2002

Charles Fierro performed in the Faculty Recital Series at California State University, Northridge on October 19th, 2002. His program was a compelling mix of masterpieces, familiar and unfamiliar, that represent a broad spectrum of piano literature. We talked with Dr. Fierro about his program.

You will open your program with* Five Pieces *by Jean-Philippe Rameau, a contemporary of Handel and J. S. Bach. Rameau was the foremost French musician of his time. What distinguishes him as a musician?

Rameau was a very respected but controversial figure in his time. The first forty years of his life were spent in obscurity as a church organist. The second half of his life brought him recognition as a theorist, court musician and composer of opera and keyboard music. He gained wide attention with the publication of his *Treatise on Harmony Reduced to its Natural Principles.* Like Paul Hindemith in the twentieth century, he sought to place the art of musical composition on a scientific foundation. "I study Nature herself—so beautiful and so simple—as a model," he wrote. He advocated the principle that melody depends on harmony, a revolutionary idea at that time. His keyboard pieces are characterized by purity of line and transparency of texture. Many of his pieces are miniature rondeaux with melodies that have the charm of French folk songs.

Beethoven's music stems from his personal struggle for self-realization and a desire to connect with his audience. How is this best illustrated in the* Sonata in D Major, op. 10, No. 3., *a work you will be performing?

When Beethoven came on the scene in Vienna he made an enormous impression. In addition to his extreme personality, he was a virtuoso pianist who enjoyed engaging people's emotions with his innovative style. He wrote music that he could perform as a calling card into high society. His *D Major Piano Sonata* of 1796 marked a highpoint in his early career. Audiences have understood that this is "*A Portrait of the Artist as a Young Man*". Each movement presents a sharply delineated aspect of Beethoven's personality. The Presto (an unusually fast tempo for a first movement) erupts into our attention the way the composer himself burst into musical society in the 1790s. Immediately he introduces the descending four-note motive that generates almost every idea in the sonata. Yet, for all its thematic richness and virtuosity, the first movement really serves as an "overture" to the Largo, which is twice as long as the other three movements combined and whose coda contains the climax of the entire sonata. In many ways, this movement anticipates a scene from the opera, *Fidelio*. The third movement, a Minuet with rustic trio, has been described by Alfred Brendel as "a gentle approach toward the warmth of the day". The fourth movement Rondo is a practical joke full of "unanswered questions" and with excursions into "dangerous" harmonic territory.

Enrique Granados'* Goyescas, *a piano suite he first performed in Barcelona in 1911, brought him worldwide recognition and enduring success. How was he inspired by the great Spanish painter Francisco Goya?

Around 1775 Goya produced thirty sketches depicting the lives of the young people of Madrid. Granados selected six of these which implied a story line about love, passion, jealousy and death. Granados was a virtuoso pianist; his composed music resembles his legendary style of improvisation. Tempos fluctuate almost constantly as he fuses Spanish melodies with Chopinesque figurations.

You will be performing the* Ballade *which is the fifth piece in the suite. Tell us about it.

The *Ballade* expertly weaves together themes from the previous four pieces, and adds an important new idea of its own. The harmonies, as well as the subtitle, *"Love and Death"*, recall the *Liebestod* from Wagner's *Tristan und Isolde.* Granados gives specific directions for the interpretation of conflicting emotions ("like happiness in the midst of sorrow") and even indicates the exact moment near the end when the young man dies after a duel. Not surprisingly, he later arranged *Goyescas* as an opera.

You have championed the music of Edward MacDowell throughout your career. In what way do you find his music compelling?

In every way: craftsmanship, imagination, directness of expression. MacDowell's music has something for every level of understanding and it is appealing to the ear. To remember MacDowell solely as the composer of *To a Wild Rose* is as unfair as remembering Beethoven solely for *Für Elise* or Brahms only for his *Lullaby.*

How would you describe MacDowell's style?

The roots of his style are firmly planted in the traditions of Mendelssohn, Schumann and Liszt; melody and character are paramount. Some aspects of his later music strike us as forward-looking and at least as modern as early Debussy. His *Twelve Virtuoso Etudes,* published in 1894, utilize chords of the seventh and ninth, a practice quite standard for the period. What is novel is his clever manner of manipulating these harmonies. He mixes major and minor modes and moves freely between sharp and flat keys. He sometimes introduces unsymmetrical sequences and irregular numbers of measures.

You have said that you perform to improve practice rather than practicing to improve performance. Please explain.

Every time we play a piece, we play it differently. Each day, new ideas, new ways of doing things, occur to us. This is true of performance as well as of practice. In a sense, the performance is just another practice session, another time through the music. Viewed in this light, the performance becomes a learning opportunity, not essentially different from what we do at home.

A View from the Footlights

"Astonish me!" Serge Diaghilev's only requirement of the composers he commissioned. The impresario knew his public. He knew they wanted to be impressed, amazed, even shocked; his taste coincided exactly with theirs. We musicians, too, need to know our audiences in order to provide them with an enjoyable experience while at the same time not going over their heads or pandering to a lowest denominator. Audiences, after all, are the lifeblood of the concert world, the prize sought competitively by managers, presenters and artists. Without audiences there would be no concerts.

Obviously, each audience is a temporary aggregate of individuals with different temperaments and backgrounds. Though no two audiences are alike, they do tend to group themselves by repertory preferences. Most classical music lovers favor standard repertory but there are significant numbers of aficionados of contemporary music, Medieval and Renaissance music, Baroque music, chamber music, sacred music, opera or a particular instrument. Of course, these groups are not mutually exclusive and there are many crossovers. A discerning audience can always distinguish between a poseur and a genuine artist, just as the collective "wisdom of crowds" has selected the best pieces to remain in the concert repertory.

In all cases, entertainment, in the highest sense of the term, is the name of the game, the "product" in the contract between performer/provider and listener/consumer. In this transaction, the artist is the expert but the audience is the judge. In preparing a performance, an experienced artist makes an educated guess about the nature of a particular audience and chooses music accordingly. In doing so, the artist assumes that the listeners are persons of friendly disposition who come there to enjoy themselves. Very likely, they already know most of the pieces on the program, at least from recordings, or else they feel genuinely curious about unfamiliar titles. (In playing for college students, I have made the mistake of believing that they are more interested in hearing modern music. Young people, I've found, are surprisingly conservative).

It may come as a surprise to some professionals that many lay listeners relate to music largely by visual imagery, metaphor or narrative, even when such associations are wildly off the mark. During a performance of an extremely intellectual mass by a fifteenth century Flemish composer, a music appreciation student remarked to me that it was like walking on a beach! Moreover, it is a commonly held view that the act of composing is a kind of psychotherapy for the expression of a composer's transitory emotional states. This is why listeners often want to know what was happening in the life of the composer while writing the piece (musicians know that this rarely has anything to do with the music). However, since music is an abstract art, visual imagery and circumstantial anecdotes, provided by program notes or pre-concert lecturers, may prove useful in pointing the listener's imagination in the right direction. There is nothing wrong with this approach, especially in the initial stages of understanding.

Audiences have a natural curiosity about performers; they want to know something about the personality and background of the soloist or group on stage but they need to take artists' bios with a grain of salt. A friend of mine attended a faculty chamber music recital at a prestigious conservatory. As a spoof of the puffery in this business, the program book listed only dreadful reviews, competitions lost, jobs not received, grants denied and promotions delayed! This negative information was just as true as the usual positive accounts intended to secure the goodwill of audiences. (The concert, by the way, was magnificent.) Of course, no one wants to read a negative bio or even a mixed one, yet an exclusively positive biography pressures an artist to live up to an irrelevant standard. In any case, bios are always about the past, sometimes the distant past. For this reason, I feel ambivalent when sending a bio to a presenter, since I want to be judged by how I play today, not by how I played last week or last year or twenty years ago.

We musicians dream of playing in halls filled with loyal listeners, and we certainly want to "please all of the people all of the time". Though we may acknowledge a secret narcissism or need for validation, mostly we just want to get the music right. We want to challenge as well as entertain, to teach while seeming not to teach. (I am aware that this statement borders on a philosophy of "edutainment".) On occasion I have encountered a subtle paradox among listeners in this country. We revere science, fund it lavishly, yet distrust erudite content in the arts. We prefer to believe that great music is a kind of accident, a by-product of momentary inspiration, innocent planning or rational structure. Even among university music majors, I have encountered the notion that knowledge is somehow antithetical to feeling.

Another challenge is the cult of the superstar. We pay top dollar to hear famous performers but fall short of supporting our regional artists in a significant, consistent manner. We even take it for granted that our musicians earn their living in some other way and should therefore provide public performances for the proverbial "modest honorarium".

In informal settings, how often have I suddenly been asked to "play something" for the amusement of guests, with blithe disregard for the long and careful preparation that must go into each and every performance! We would not make a similar demand of any other professional. At social gatherings nowadays, I'm tempted to tell people I am a psychiatrist!

Probably the greatest challenge an artist confronts is the oversupply of professional musicians. There can never be too many amateurs, but apparently there can be too many professionals in a given market. For the freelance performer lucky enough to obtain a concert contract, the chances of securing a second engagement from a presenting organization are small, regardless of how successful the performance is, because literally thousands of performers eagerly offer their services for a lower fee. This unhealthy situation may appear to be good for consumers in the short run but proves destructive for musicians, and consequently for music, in the long term. Contrary to myth, desperation and unemployment are not good for art or artists. Music, like any human endeavor, can flourish only when musicians enjoy economic stability.

As we drive to a concert, we see people in their cars going some other place but not to the concert. Within a mile of the recital hall, we pass hundreds of homes whose residents have no idea that a musical event is taking place practically in their own backyards. As we step onto the stage and look across the footlights to the audience, we sincerely appreciate their presence; we feel their warm regard and support. We want to touch their minds with noble music, not merely "astonish" them. We also want to help them understand our work and we want to extend our service to people who are not there.

Fall 2004

Turning the Tables

Most musicians would agree that the center of our musical life is practice. Here is the activity where we engage the art most personally, the place where we spend the bulk of our musical time.

When we practice we literally create a virtual reality, an alternate world both beautiful and challenging. Our involvement with it brings us totally into the present, evoking a sustained pleasurable response. The practice hour becomes not merely an escape from daily concerns but an end in itself, worth doing for its own sake.

When a concert date approaches, however, our attention suddenly shifts to the performance. The future event becomes our goal, practice merely a means.

To be sure, a committed performance date motivates us, concentrates our mind and encourages efficiency. "As we practice, so we will play." But when we allow the performance to turn into the Big Event, the test of our preparation, the game changes. The concert becomes the reason to practice; inspiration and pleasure diminish.

To restore balance, I have found it helpful to invert the equation. Now, instead of practicing to improve performance, I perform to improve practice! Here's my rationale. Every time we play a piece, we play it differently. Each day, new ideas, new ways of doing things, occur to us. This is true of performance as well as of practice. In a sense, the performance is just another practice session, another time through the music. Viewed in this light, the performance becomes a learning opportunity, not essentially different from what we do at home. Sometimes, in advance of a concert, various concerns crowd my mind. Will the piano on stage have a difficult action? Will the audience be responsive? Will my performance stand up to being recorded, broadcast or reviewed in the press? But then I remember why I scheduled the concert in the first place. I remind myself that I am on stage to enjoy learning. Then I can focus on the thing that matters most: the music. This change of thinking not only depressurizes the performance, it opens my mind to spur-of-the-moment ideas. (This is what is meant by "inspiration".) I find myself playing with the music. I try new phrasing, experiment with pedaling, risk a more dramatic accent here, a bolder *ritard* there. In a word, I begin "practicing" on stage. No longer concerned with reproducing exactly what I learned at home, I experience the familiar pleasure of creating.

Heightened awareness during performance gives us valuable insights about our playing which we can use to improve our practice skills. Tempo management, concentration on musical character, maintaining the "long line", are things I've learned on stage. I now apply them consciously and consistently in practice. The stage is our best teacher because it shows us how to practice better.

Next time you play for people, turn the tables! Make creative discovery the focus of your performance, just as you do in practice. You may be surprised how much you enjoy performing!

Fall 1999

Playing for Beethoven

Have you ever wondered what it would be like to perform Beethoven's music for Beethoven himself? What would he want from our interpretations? We know, of course, that he insisted on fidelity to the score but we also know that he demanded a strong imaginative approach.

In his book, *The Sonatas of Beethoven as He Played and Taught Them*, Kenneth Drake gives a remarkable list of adjectives used by Beethoven's pupil, Carl Czerny, to illustrate that character delineation is primary in performing Beethoven's music. There can be no doubt that Czerny heard these words from the master himself. A few examples: grand, religious, tragic, intimate, flattering, noisy, exalted, teasing, dreamy, naïve, serious, sensitive, peaceful, singing. I never played for Beethoven, of course, but my experience in playing for living composers is similar: they want us to bring conviction, ideas and a point of view to our performance, not just to play "correctly". As students, we learn the principles of pianism and musicianship (relax the wrist, "hear" the note in your mind before you leap to it, give the rests full value etc.). Our teachers also transmit to us the traditions of style (where to play freely or strictly, whether to pedal or not). More importantly, they demonstrate insight, the power to "read between the lines", to understand the why behind the notes. Our instructors model this skill and eventually we learn how to do it on our own.

Development of insight is greatly assisted by the technique of structural hearing (developed by Heinrich Schenker and Felix Salzer) that reveals organic sense and does not merely count notes or label chords. Insight also comes from a poetic approach that goes directly to musical meaning.

I vividly recall playing a piece by Ingolf Dahl for the composer himself. About a certain phrase he said, "It should sound like a tree in a fog." Immediately and without further practice, my muscular coordination altered to produce the magical sound of the passage.

Most of the music we play has its own emotive associations, references and suggestions. Metaphorical thinking unlocks memories of these emotions and makes it possible for us to communicate artistically with other human beings. How do we access these feelings? How do we know what the music is "about"? I believe we do this through imagination, the ability to make connections between life and art. Imagination goes beyond the technical and intellectual sides of music and seeks the subtext. This intuitive process may happen spontaneously but can also be developed consciously.

The second movement of Beethoven's *Piano Sonata in B-flat Major, op. 22,* will illuminate this thought. Here we have a conventional formal plan with straightforward harmonic organization. The melodic lines tend to be florid and wide-ranging, the accompaniments chordal with occasional contrapuntal motion, all moving in a steady 9/8 *adagio*. The pedaling requires sensitivity, otherwise the piece places no unusual requirements on the pianist.

But what is it all about? What does Beethoven mean when he asks us to play *con molto espressione?* Of course, there are many possible answers but if we see that the music is in the style of a serenade, a love song with a promise of happiness and the hope of overcoming future difficulties, then we have a plausible scenario, a reason why the music is as it is. The *appoggiaturas* will sigh with longing, the *sforzandos* will wound, the resolutions will console and the recapitulation will vibrate with optimism. Very importantly, these perceptions color the sound quality we choose for the expression of the piece. Moreover, since many of the melodic dissonances occur on the first beat of the measure, we now perceive that the accompanying chords move urgently toward the following downbeats (8-9-1). This may not be the only way to read this sonata movement but it offers a coherent point of view on which to build an interpretation in which every choice of tempo, dynamics and phrasing will contribute to the total effect.

For years, Beethoven contemplated re-publishing all his earlier works with the addition of descriptive and poetic titles. In the end he wisely decided against it. By specifying mood or character to such an extent, he would have limited the performer's powers of free association. Chopin and Brahms resisted the same temptation. The fanciful names in some editions of Mendelssohn's *Songs without Words* (originally called *Preludes)* are not by the composer but were added by publishers to promote sales. Significantly, Debussy places the titles of his *Preludes* after three dots, in parentheses, and at the end of each piece. He wanted to direct the imagination of players in a characteristically understated way.

Does the metaphorical approach work for music from all historical periods? Certainly, it applies best to nineteenth-century works, where literary, narrative or pictorial aspects lie just below the surface. In a sense, the entire Romantic repertory consists of songs without words. Prior to that time, instrumental music was more about movement than about meaning, as critic Henry Pleasants observes. With the pre-Romantic *Sturm und Drang* crisis of the 1760s and its emphasis on personal emotion, the role of the performer gradually changed from Executant to Interpreter, and the subjective expression that characterizes vocal music entered instrumental music. This is why many of Mozart's piano pieces have a kinship to his operas and why it pays to compare the words and dramatic situations of the arias with the music of the sonata or concerto at hand.

Ideally, interpreting contemporary music should come naturally for us because it is of our own time, though the styles may be new and unfamiliar. Some modern composers choose to eliminate extra-musical suggestions entirely, creating patterns that move exclusively in intervals of sound and time. Yet for musicians of a "romantic" temperament, it seems that even works of "absolute" music come from memories of common experience and these connections need to be sought if we want to project the music in a way that people will understand. Arnold Schoenberg said that there are no modern pieces, only bad performances. I believe he was not criticizing players' deficiency of skill, but rather their lack of associative emotional thinking.

In 1980 I had the privilege of participating in Aaron Copland's eightieth birthday concert by performing his *Piano Quartet* (1950) with three excellent string players. As we played it for the composer, we were impressed by how much he wanted us to project the character of the music; in fact, he used some of the same imagery that Czerny used. It was like playing for Beethoven.

Winter 2004

Building an Interpretation

Great music is open to infinite interpretations. Some of these interpretations strike us as more authentic, more convincing than others. As performers, we want to know a composer's intentions as best we can; at the same time, we want our reading of a piece to ring true for us and our listeners.

Because music is an abstract art, we need all the help we can get in understanding it. For me, the most important resource in developing an interpretation is imagination. I have written about this subject previously in these pages.

Another resource is analysis, by which we bring our knowledge of functional harmony and musical architecture to an understanding of the place and direction of every note and phrase in an entire composition. This scientific, rational approach does not inhibit spontaneous performance, but liberates it. It clarifies content, distinguishing the more significant from the less important, the transitions from the goals, the valleys from the peaks. As Paul Hindemith observed, the mysteries of music lie in its meaning, not in its processes.

Thoughtful repetitive practice can also reveal meaning because we often find that the answer to a technical problem lies in a musical solution.

I like to use music to explain music. Rather than discuss "influence", I prefer to talk about context. Every piece comes from somewhere; it has "ancestors", "siblings", "cousins" and "descendants". These shed light on each other. (This is one of the benefits of a comprehensive recital.) A startlingly original composer like Beethoven, for example, makes even more sense when we see the daring innovations of C. P. E. Bach and Haydn. Schubert's song texts help us understand his solo keyboard music. Liszt's extravagant pianistic gestures predict and legitimize the coloristic writing in Ravel. A study of Schoenberg's music elucidates our comprehension of Brahms. There is hardly anything new under the sun. Serial writing has antecedents in the ground basses and *ricercari* of Purcell and Froberger, not to mention canons by Bach and his predecessors. Renaissance madrigals and African drumming patterns reappear in new form in Ligeti, and the principle of perpetual variation organizes music of the most disparate styles and periods.

In creating a context, it is helpful to know as much music as we can, not only the acknowledged masterpieces, but also folk music and works by less famous composers. (A true topography of the earth has to account for all of its features, not only those above 10,000 feet.) Such a study provides a standard for comparison. It illuminates the multi-dimensional relationships of music from different times. Our purpose, however, is not to catalog the external functions of our art, but to use these to arrive at its interior motivations. That is what interpretation is.

Summer 2006

To Memorize or Not

For amateur musicians, one major concern, beyond technique and interpretation, is the question of performance from memory. Probably no other single factor elicits more apprehension before and uneasiness during a concert.

I've known students for whom public performance is the simplest thing in the world; never a worry, never a need to try out the instrument or review the score before walking out on stage. All they have to do is show up at the piano and the notes pour out from their fingers in a kind of digital ecstasy with total reliability every time. (Musical insight or the conveying of deeper layers of meaning is another matter.)

On the other hand, I knew a pianist whose performances of any repertory, Bach, Mozart, Schubert, Liszt, and especially Chopin, were extraordinary. Her commanding sound at the instrument, her dramatic projection of phrasing, her genius for pedaling and color, and above all, her musical ideas, electrify me even today, decades after hearing them. Yet she chose not to pursue a concert career because of occasional memory lapses in performance. The world was needlessly deprived of hearing this great artist.

Since the time of Franz Liszt, it has been traditional for professionals to perform everything from memory. This is expected at all competitions and is one of the requirements for a degree in music. Memorizing is good because it makes us pay attention to details, analyze every move and understand harmonic and structural processes. Moreover, the thoughtful repetition involved in memorizing deepens our understanding of the music.

However, memorizing and performing from memory are two different things. For some musicians, playing from memory enhances freedom and inspiration in performance, for others, it may produce the opposite effect. If we perform some pieces better from memory, we certainly should do so. If we perform better and feel more confident with the score on the music desk, we should do that. We ought not to be deterred from performance by whether or not there is a piece of paper in front of us. Whether we choose to use the score or perform from memory, it is important to make the decision well in advance of the concert so that we practice in the manner we will perform. If a memory problem occurs during a memorized solo recital, it affects only one player. Chamber music, however, is almost always performed with the score in order to facilitate the complex interaction among the players. Logically, the same principle should apply in concertos, though custom dictates that the soloist performs from memory to emphasize the contrast between the individual and the group and to enhance audience excitement by removing the performer's safety net.

I have come to the conviction that the quality of our experience (how we feel) during performance is important and that we should not devalue our personal emotional state while we are on stage. After all, our primary purpose in performing is to make music, not to show off our memory skills or tolerance for pressure. For career pianists, performance from memory is a grand tradition and a matter of professional pride. For amateurs, would it not be better to deliver an integral, confident performance while using the score, rather than endure anxiety or risk derailment while performing by heart?

We know that Beethoven performed his own concertos from the manuscript because Carl Czerny reports turning pages for the master. Clara Schumann reports that in her early career, she was criticized for not using the score in performance. The great artists whom we admire have played their repertory hundreds of times on tour, yet even they have occasional memory problems. The legendary British pianist, Myra Hess, always used the score in concert, in order to assure that she was delivering all the details of the music. Among performers today, Mitsuko Uchida, Alicia de Larrocha and Ivo Pogorelich play everything from memory but the original Finnish pianist, Olli Mustonen, sometimes uses the score. Christopher Taylor and David Burge perform avant-garde music from memory while Maurizio Pollini and Alfred Brendel play the standard repertory from memory, but use the score in modern works, with the assistance of a deft page-turner.

I, myself, have tried it both ways. In my experience, it depends partly on the degree of chromaticism and registral discontinuity in the composition, but mostly it depends on the length of time I can devote to learning the music. Is it worth a year of work to solidify the memorization of a piece that we could play equally well from the score with half the preparation time? If we work long enough, we can memorize anything, even irrational music. But at what price? For each of us, time is a diminishing, non-renewable resource. How many more concerts could we play if we gave ourselves permission to use the score on stage? If doing so would have a positive effect on the result, perhaps the time has come to question the belief that we must always perform everything from memory. For all artists, the primary emphasis has to be on musical values. This is why we play and why the audience comes to the concert. Our pleasure in performing contributes importantly to the quality of our work and to our life experience. Whatever helps us play better and feel better is the right thing for us, for the audience and for the music.

Spring 2004

Reckoning with Records

During the intermission of a recital by a famous pianist, I overheard someone say, "Great performance! Just like a CD!" No doubt, the listener intended the comment as high praise, but I was taken aback by the idea that a derivative medium could be regarded as the standard for a live experience. Imagine admiring a masterpiece in a museum and remarking, "Great painting! Just like a photo reprint!"

The educational value of recordings has been apparent ever since Thomas Edison invented the phonograph in 1889. The new technology provided unprecedented access to music from all periods and cultures. Today, in the comfort of our living rooms, the world's finest musicians play for us, and best of all, we can hear historical performances by legendary artists of the early twentieth century.

It is tempting to attribute a certain authority to discs and tapes. After all, we reason, if a performance is recorded, it must be "right". But this is as illogical as saying that something is true simply because it appears in print. A microphone registers sound; it cannot create truth. As music lovers, we seek performances that are "definitive"; we want to know how the music is "supposed" to go. Masterpieces, however, are inexhaustible: there is always more that can be discovered, more that can be understood. All performances of great music are provisional.

One day, I tuned in to a classical music radio station during the broadcast of a familiar piano piece. There were several places in the music where I thought, "I would never do it that way!" You may imagine my surprise when the host announced that it was my performance, recorded a year earlier! In the intervening time, my ideas about the music had evolved, but the recording had not. This is why a conductor friend of mine believes that CDs should self-destruct after three playings!

To be convincing, an interpretation must be authentic, that is, personal. This is our responsibility as artists. Insights may arrive by inspiration, but more often they have to be earned by prolonged questioning of the score. While teaching at the university, I could always tell when students had gotten an interpretive idea from a recording instead of arriving at it themselves. In fact, I could often tell which recording they had been listening to. Certainly, we can profit from listening to recorded performances, but the right time to study them is after we have formed our own ideas about a piece, when we have established a personal point of view about the music. If we listen too soon, how can we learn to trust ourselves or develop independent interpretive powers? According to Robert Schumann, a good musician understands a score without hearing it performed. Similarly, a good musician can interpret a score without listening to a CD.

Recordings and live performances, though using the same music, are actually distinct art forms because we listen differently in different situations. The acoustical space in a concert hall is exponentially greater than our space at home or in a car, and this fact materially alters our perception of the music. At home we listen alone or with a handful of people, whereas the company of a large audience in a hall psychologically affects our experience. I have attended a concert, then heard it again later on a broadcast and not recognized the event. It "feels" different.

More important for both artist and audience is the absolute uniqueness of a live performance. A live performance is always and only "in the moment", entailing inspiration and risk; next time it will be different, no matter how much control we exert. A recording, even of an inspired performance, is obviously stable and repeatable. Once we have heard it, even the noblest idea becomes predictable; minor flaws and extraneous sounds become anticipated and magnified. This is why editing of studio recordings is necessary.

However, editing creates an expectation of superhuman perfection that is carried unconsciously into the concert hall by both players and listeners. For the performer, this situation is detrimental and inartistic. Nowadays, many young players work toward a kind of technical reliability that minimizes the possibility of discovery in performance. But is it not the prospect of such revelation that prompts us to attend a concert in the first place?

"I had to learn to play the piano three times", declared Artur Schnabel; "first, to play the piano; second, to play for an audience; third, to play for a microphone." Because microphones pick up and exaggerate transient noises from the instrument, pianists need to modify touch and pedal technique in order to avoid undesirable percussive effects. Also, experienced artists like to record in long "takes" in order to create a gestalt, an organic sense of spontaneity, coherence and line. They do not rely on a patchwork of splices to make themselves sound better than they really are.

When we purchase a CD, there are many things we are paying not to know. Almost every recording session has its own tale of mishaps and near-disasters, more humorous in the re-telling than in the actual event. A perfectly fine piano can suddenly decide to break a hammer. A *coloratura* cricket can start singing somewhere in the rafters. At one of my sessions, a crucial piece of electronic equipment failed; back-ups were not available because it was a holiday weekend. My most successful recording had to be made at 5:00 a.m., the only time the studio was available! (I can still hear the grumbling of the technicians and engineers.)

Funding can be a mixed blessing. Given the limited public appetite for art music, record companies sometimes have to subsidize their classical music projects by budget transfers from their popular music divisions. Although foundations do a great deal to encourage the arts, they are famously slow and they like to spread grants thinly among many applicants. On one of my recordings, we encountered a number of expensive mechanical problems, so that the entire budget ran out during the editing of the first piece. We had to abandon the project for a year and return to fundraising.

Like everything else, the repertory on records is determined largely by the market or by a company director's hunch about what consumers will buy. This accounts for the lopsided representation of warhorses in the Schwann catalog and the absence of superb recordings by artists who are "unknown". Paradoxically, in this business you have to be famous before you can be successful. With today's technology, an individual artist can produce a high quality disc with private funds, but to achieve wider distribution, an artist needs a record company. However, even major labels are at the mercy of retailers. If a disc doesn't sell in three weeks, it disappears from the shelves. If it does well in the marketplace, the bulk of the proceeds goes to the middle people, the artist receiving only pennies per unit sold. Notwithstanding these observations, recordings have become an indispensable means of enlightenment and communication. They contribute to our enjoyment of life and transmit culture by showing us what other musicians think about the repertory. For artists themselves, recordings are an ideal way to document their careers and provide an enduring legacy to the world.

Fall 2003

Confessions of an Adjudicator

For pianists planning to enter a competition and for music lovers generally, it might be interesting to know what goes through the minds of adjudicators and what their backstage discussions are like.

A certain excitement surrounds a performance or competition because music, like drama, is an art that unfolds moment by moment. We cannot know for sure how we will play, no matter how well prepared we may be (This is true even when we play for ourselves at home.) The unknown, therefore, is inherent in the nature of music itself and since we are fallible beings, a flair for the moment, a sense of humor, is essential for any performer.

The judges know this because they are usually concert artists themselves; often they are teachers of long experience and persons of integrity who are selected for their broad knowledge of the repertory. Though individual adjudicators come from different backgrounds, it is remarkable how often they reach consensus, if not always unanimity. They take their responsibilities seriously, often serving pro bono, or receiving at most, a modest honorarium. Adjudicators who have worked with a competitor should disqualify themselves to avoid conflict of interest or the appearance of impropriety.

More than anything, judges seek to uphold the standards of the art. At the same time, they are keenly aware of their own limitations and frailties. Whenever disaster can befall a pianist during performance, it has probably happened to the judges at one time or another. Consequently, judges tend to bring a generous supply of empathy to their task.

Adjudicators are basically listeners and the first thing that strikes a listener's ear is tone quality. At a competition or jury, it is amazing how utterly different the same instrument can sound in the hands of a succession of players! Still, some basic issues typically arise. Does the sound "project", even at the softest dynamic levels? Are the *fortes* rich without pounding? Is the pianist listening for the continuation of sound in harmonic suspensions and *cantabile* passages? Do the inner voices and accompaniments have vitality of their own? Does the player distinguish between *piano* and *mezzo piano* or between *forte* and *fortissimo* and recreate the identical sound level in parallel places elsewhere in the piece? In other words, does the pianist understand the structural significance of dynamics?

It's the player's responsibility to engage and maintain the listener's attention. Ideally, the music should seem to be created on the spot. I am often struck by how quickly performers reveal their musical profiles. Nonetheless, an experienced adjudicator is not swayed by first impressions, but allows for different aspects of the pianist's personality to emerge later in the program.

Where competitors have the option to select their own pieces, adjudicators are looking for appropriateness of repertory, music that shows the contestant's unique qualities while allowing a margin of comfort that makes for graceful delivery. No one enjoys hearing a musician struggling with the score or barely surviving the performance. Paradoxically, at any level of advancement, we are always dealing with the fundamentals. Sensitive response to the size and direction of intervals, to harmonic events and rates of change, clear distinction between upbeats and downbeats, the rhetorical power of rests and *fermatas,* the pacing of *ritardandos,* all these apply equally to a Haydn minuet and a Rachmaninoff concerto.

Choice of tempo is the factor that most directly affects musical character, as well as the delivery of details and the psychological security of the player. But stability of tempo is equally important. Even in Romantic music, the temporal freedom makes sense only if the underlying metric pulse is firm. Inaccurate observation of note values and liberties that occur too often not only destabilize rhythm, they actually undermine musical meaning. A discerning musician knows that a single, strategically placed *rubato* is more effective than a series of small ones. Musical education enhances awareness as much as it develops proficiency. An intelligent performer investigates how music is put together, from detail to grand design, and wants above all to maintain the long line that vivifies a piece. Musicians who integrate theoretical knowledge with performance skills understand how composers, especially from the eighteenth century, play with our expectations, intentionally misleading in order to surprise us.

Beyond technical security and fidelity to the score, adjudicators are listening for an expressive performance, one that identifies the character of the music and shows commitment to it. "I cannot move others unless I myself am moved", said Beethoven. This requires the player to exercise insight, to read between the lines and convey the subtext convincingly in a personal way without exaggeration. Of all the musical sins, a few wrong notes are far less offensive than a lack of feeling.

Colleagues who have participated in international competitions report that contestants must maintain a large quantity of diverse repertory in top condition, and that the performance sometimes takes place on an unfamiliar piano without benefit of tryout. It is our bane as pianists that we have to play the instrument that is there. On pianos whose dampers cut off the sound abruptly, the keys should be released more gradually than usual.

Contestants are often concerned about being compared to other pianists, especially on a point system. My teacher, Adele Marcus, used to say that this is a comparative world. We prefer pianist X for certain pieces and pianist Y for others; nobody is great in everything. Competition rules require that judges rank the contestants. However, I confess that, in adjudicating, I decline to assign a numerical value to matters such as phrasing and interpretation.

Among young musicians, there is a common misconception that winning a competition virtually guarantees a career. I hasten to emphasize that competitions have no such power. At major events, medalists receive exposure and performance opportunities for a limited time. After that, most disappear from public view as next year's winners arrive on an overcrowded concert scene. Competitors do well to remember that their true reward is the self-improvement that has already resulted from their additional preparation. In the end, what really matters is our ability to have a normal musical life, to practice every day, teach, to compose, to make chamber music with our friends. In such a musical life, everyone is a winner.

Spring 2003

Recovery

It was one of those glorious autumn mornings in Southern California: hillsides painted brilliant green by a recent storm; a deep blue, almost purple sky; a warm, fragrant breeze; crystalline views of the San Gabriel Mountains covered with snow. As I went for a walk to enjoy the splendid scene, I tripped on a concrete obstruction. X-rays at the hospital showed that the fall had crushed my left wrist; the orthopedist prescribed a surgical implant and a long period of recuperation with no guarantee of success.

How does a pianist confront such news? As an experienced hiker and temperamentally risk-averse individual, I am the last person in the world to whom this accident should happen. The fact that it occurred not on some peak in the Sierras or the Alps but a few yards from my home makes it even more unlikely. Would I be able to play the piano again? If so, when and at what level?

But these were longer-term questions. First came the struggle of coping with daily life on a one-handed basis. The simplest tasks, like tying shoelaces, required assistance from others. (Try peeling a banana with one hand!) Driving became especially risky and inadvisable.

I like to think that the universe is unfolding precisely as it should. Still, three years after the incident, I do not (yet) see a purpose in it. Human nature, however, tends to draw good from evil; maybe there was something to be learned here. I found that people are more generous than I had ever imagined. The support and practical help I received from my sister, Nancy, and many friends demonstrated in a tangible way that friends in need are friends indeed.

During the process of rehabilitation, atrophy proved to be the biggest challenge. Stabilization of a limb in a cast quickly causes muscular deterioration, while progress in occupational therapy moves at an infinitesimally slow pace, requiring tenacity familiar from a lifetime of music study. Classical pianists know from experience how to overcome frustration and to persist, no matter what.

We musicians live a hurry-hurry existence: always so much to do, yet quality in performance takes forever to achieve. (*Ars longa; vita brevis,* the ancient Romans used to say.) This is why the mishap felt like a colossal loss of irretrievable time. Simultaneously there appeared an unaccustomed quantity of empty temporal space to fill. What to do with it? I tackled this question by temporarily switching hats: my new "job" was to attend therapy sessions nine hours a week and to accomplish the assigned exercises at home. These included flexion and extension of the wrist while wearing a custom-designed dynamic splint. After several months of work, I regained some range of motion and could practice Hanon studies slowly at the piano. This represented an encouraging advancement, now that I could place my hand on the keyboard in a prone (palm downward) position.

During the year of recovery, I studied repertory away from the piano and pursued a lifelong interest in classical Greek literature. I taught master classes, provided consultations and adjudications and wrote articles, typing on the computer keyboard with one hand. I learned that life is bigger than music or career and that I "am" not a pianist, but a human being who plays the piano. Having to live for a long period without actively making music, I found that I could still be happy.

Throughout the course of recuperation, I received care from specialists of extraordinary dedication and ethical standards.

My social horizon broadened. Some fellow patients, mostly non-musicians, had suffered injuries greater than mine. They had sought second and third opinions, filled out countless bureaucratic forms, undergone multiple surgeries and procedures and endured interminable waits in medical offices. They persevered in physical therapy, sometimes for years. The example of these brave individuals increased my patience in general.

I resolved to use the recovery time wisely and to benefit other musicians whenever possible. Above all, I determined to return to the concert stage. Now that I have done so, it is a special pleasure to play the piano.

Winter 2008

In Praise of Amateurs

"It is a good thing that people are willing to pay me for playing the piano," declared Artur Rubinstein; if they weren't, I would do it anyway!" The great pianist knew intuitively that music is worth doing for the psychic benefits it provides.

Researchers have shown that playing the piano stimulates imagination and develops neuromuscular coordination, but the real reason we play the piano is that it promotes happiness. Playing an instrument fills a human need to encounter challenges and to create something beautiful, an activity that enhances emotional health. (It is also a fact that happy human beings are more likely to live responsibly in society.) As philosopher George Santayana observed, "The purpose of art is to make life better."

Composers wrote some of their most beautiful music specifically for amateurs. The Chopin mazurkas, the Schubert waltzes, many pieces by Bach, Haydn, Mozart, Grieg, MacDowell, Tchaikovsky and Bartok come to mind. There was a time when almost every home had a piano and someone there could play Mendelssohn's *Songs Without Words.*

An amateur is a person who cultivates a particular pursuit without a professional purpose. I like the term as it is used in sports, where it does not suggest a lack of skill, but the status of one who plays without renumeration. (Olympic athletes, the best in the world, are amateurs.) Professionals may have more experience with the piano, the repertory and the performing situation, but amateurs enjoy a certain advantage: they are free from the constraints and compromises of concert artists. They can devote their attention entirely to the music without concern for sensation-seeking presenters and the tyranny of the bottom line.

For amateurs and professionals alike, it is always a good idea to give a recital. The prospect of public performance motivates us to prepare more effectively and to develop our skills. In the absolute sense, it makes no difference whether we perform in Vienna or Van Nuys, the criterion of quality resides in the music itself and is the same for everyone, everywhere. As Artur Schnabel said, “Masterpieces are better than any performance of them”, so there is always room for improvement in our interpretation.

Because the piano is a one-person “orchestra” that can deliver a complete composition without the assistance of other musicians, it carries an occupational hazard: isolation. String players, wind players and singers almost always rehearse in the company of other musicians, a situation both corrective and supportive. This is why it is important for pianists to play with and for other musicians, to augment the number of ears and ideas in the room. I have long advocated the formation of Piano Clubs to compensate for isolation and to foster a sense of community among pianists. We need to feel that other pianists support our work, that they wish us well and that we do the same for them.

After all, we are colleagues and the number of performances by friends in libraries, churches, schools and private homes is cause for rejoicing. There can never be too many amateurs because as pianist Ruth Slenczynska remarked, “There can never be too much beauty in the world.”

Summer 2003

A Musical Discovery—Ashot Zohrabian

The world premiere of an important piece of music is always a cause for celebration, and when the work itself is particularly distinguished, there is special reason to rejoice. Just such an occasion occurred on March 19, 2010 at Zipper Hall in Los Angeles when the Dilijan Concerts presented the newly commissioned *Novelette* by Ashot Zohrabian.

Zohrabian, 65, is one of the most esteemed composers in Armenia. He has had numerous successful performances internationally. Listeners everywhere find that his music is a discovery well worth making.

A survey of his catalog reveals an allegiance to chamber music, and the *Novelette* is in fact a piano quartet structured as a single movement. Zohrabian's harmonic idiom is personal and at the same time completely comprehensible. The music has a narrative, almost autobiographical quality, communicating intense emotions with remarkable transparency.

Audiences expect music by Armenian composers to "sound Armenian" while simultaneously embracing Western stylistic advances, a challenge that Zohrabian met without pastiche or compromise. After a single hearing, it would be premature to proclaim this as a masterpiece, but we have the sense that this work is a major contribution to the chamber music repertory and that it will merit many performances.

The program opened with the early *String Quartet in E-flat Major* by Franz Schubert, followed by *Four Bagatelles for String Quartet* by the independent Armenian-American composer Alan Hovhaness (1911-2000), whose fascination with philosophies of the Far East inspired him to create music of a mystical persuasion. Broad tempos and slow harmonic progressions seem to suspend the flow of time and induce a mood of stillness and contemplation.

The concert concluded with one of the summits of the Romantic period, the *Concerto for Violin, Piano and String Quartet* by the French composer, Ernest Chausson (1855-1899). Chausson came from a cultured, privileged background and throughout his life maintained connections with the literary salons of the day. Occasionally his style reminds us of the music of his teacher, Cesar Franck, from whom he inherited a penchant for frequent modulations and cyclical forms. One observer has remarked that if Marcel Proust had written music, it might have sounded like Chausson: opulent, passionate and meticulous.

In the Dilijan Concert tradition, all the performances were superb. Members of the Apple Hill String Quartet (Elise Kuder, Sarah Kim, Mike Kelly and Rupert Thompson) displayed admirable ensemble cohesiveness and dedication to the music. Violinist Movses Pogossian and pianist Gavin Martin brought all their resources of elegant virtuosity and insight to their roles. Altogether it was a memorable concert experience.

Spring 2010

Afterthoughts I

Posts to the Editor

Throughout his long history with Piano Forte *newsletter, Charles was thoroughly engaged with every issue and after reading it he would email me his comments. I was very appreciative of his observations and offer excerpts that shine light on his dedication to the music that filled his life.*

"I read the article by Saint-Saens four or five times and was surprised to discover that even as late as 1910, the orchestral tone poems by Liszt had not yet achieved the public acclaim they deserve. It was also illuminating to see what one great composer thought about another great composer and who even took on the responsibility to gather an orchestra (and presumably also to finance it) to conduct those works. It was a rare tribute. Liszt himself was also a generous person, tirelessly promoting the music of Bach and Schubert and making piano arrangements of the Beethoven symphonies and writing piano arrangements of famous arias by Verdi. In our time, Hindemith was the soloist in the *Viola Concerto* by William Walton. It is nice to learn about the cooperative efforts of musicians."

"I especially liked the interview with Leonid Hambro. I was a guest on his radio program once. He told me another story about playing a Hindemith concerto with the composer conducting in New York. Robb Martson, whom you have interviewed, was one of the pianists touring with the Hambro Piano Quartet."

"Thank you for publishing my article about MacDowell's *Sonata Eroica*. As you know, I have been involved with the music of this composer for many years, in performances, tours, lectures and recordings. It is one of my goals to bring public attention and appreciation to this great music; the appearance of the article in your Newsletter will certainly enhance these efforts."

"I especially appreciated the thought-provoking essay by Rachmaninoff, in particular the paragraph about iconoclasm as the law of artistic progress, and his insistence that musicians must find what gives a musical work unity, cohesion, force and grace."

"I found your editorial about mental discipline in managing distractions particularly valuable. The art of extended concentration is more valuable than ever nowadays. I've learned that keeping the phone in a different room, away from the piano, helps a lot."

"The letter from the young Prokofiev is charming! It reveals much about the behind-the-scenes atmosphere, procedures and personalities at the Russian conservatory. From my years of administering entrance auditions at CSUN, I see that 'the more things change, the more they stay the same.' "

"I liked very much the article comparing Scriabin and Rachmaninoff, as well as the biography and interview with Ornela Ervin, whom I have met several times, but am only now learning about her background. My favorite article in this issue is your editorial. You have eloquently explained the connection between musical study and personal fulfillment. I find that, after a lifetime of dedication to music, it is still very challenging, and that this is the reason to keep doing it. Risk and courage are part of the growth process."

Reviews

Although these reviews are not part of the Piano Forte *article collection, I wanted to share them with you as they form part of Charles' body of writing and reveal him as a critical and observant listener.*

A Very Special Concert: Music of Arno Babadjanian

In art as in life, things rarely go perfectly, but when they do, we feel lucky indeed. Just such a fortunate occasion took place in Los Angeles at a concert presented by the Dilijan Music Society. A capacity audience gathered at the Herbert Zipper Hall for a program of chamber music by Arno Babadjanian (1921-1983). The late composer enjoyed the status of a national hero in his native Armenia and in Soviet Russia, where he received numerous honors, awards and commissions. His compositions are well known in communities of the Armenian diaspora; outside these communities, however, he has yet to receive recognition he deserves.

The quality of at least two of the selections on the program demonstrated conclusively that his is a major talent. The late *Third String Quartet* (1979) employs avant-garde idioms with telling effect. Within a tight structure, the music commands attention from beginning to end of its single-movement design.

Similarly, the virtuosic early *Piano Trio* (1952), displays mastery of all its musical elements in a striking way and, in the opinion of some musicologists, raised the art of Armenian chamber music to a new level.

It is important to remember that Babadjanian's entire career took place during the Soviet era, when state sponsorship and state control imposed a Socialist Realist doctrine on all the arts. Creative minds responded to these strictures in varying ways. We remember the bitter ironies and pseudo-conformities of Shostakovich and Prokofiev. Babadjanian found his own way, sometimes sincerely producing music that would appeal to a mass public, at other times, as in the *Third String Quartet*, asserting astonishing modernist independence.

Four Songs for soprano and piano, in a style somewhere between Rachmaninoff and Jerome Kern, illustrated the composer's successful attempt to achieve the warmth and immediacy of popular music. *The Poem* (1966) for solo piano showed the composer beginning to fuse serial techniques with traditional ethnic idioms. During an interview in lieu of intermission, the distinguished composer, Tigran Mansurian, shared reminiscences of his friendship with his senior colleague.

The performers, all well-known to Southern California audiences, were superb. Violinists Roger Wilkie and Movses Pogossian, violist Kate Vincent, cellist Ronald Leonard and soprano Maria Abajan, projected their respective roles with consummate skill and sensitivity. The big find of the day was guest pianist Artur Avanesov. His formidable technical prowess, dramatic insight and engaging personality were important factors in making this a memorable event. I hope he will return often.

Dmitry Rachmanov in Scriabin CSUN Cypress Recital Hall

September 28, 2013

It was a historic moment in the history of the CSUN Music Department when Professor Dmitry Rachmanov played an all-Scriabin piano recital on September 28. A capacity audience turned out for the rare opportunity to hear a comprehensive survey of music by this major Russian composer performed by a world class Russian pianist. This was Rachmanov at his best, and as we approach the centenary of the Russian composer's death, it was particularly important that we hear his music at this time.

The program followed a generally chronological line from the composer's early Chopinesque period through the mystical and visionary late works. Scriabin was not only a one-man history of music at the turn of the twentieth century: he was one of its major driving forces. His innovations in harmony, form, pianism and philosophy remain vital today.

In a survey of preludes, etudes, character pieces and four sonatas from every period of Scriabin's short life (1872-1915), the pianist revealed that even at the beginning, Scriabin was already an independent spirit and became increasingly daring as he progressed. At all times, as he advanced the coloristic resources of the piano, he discovered new psychological and emotional territory. Words like "intimate, impulsive, imperious, menacing, vaporous, impassioned, despairing, heartbreaking" appear in his scores. With juxtapositions of such extreme variety, the musical structures run the risk of flying apart, but through sheer passion, technical brilliance and intellectual control, Rachmanov made the music totally coherent and poetic.

Amid the florid writing he expressed the melodic lines that are the heart of the music, delivering the extravagant piano writing with breathtaking artistic command.

Rachmanov's performance was more than a recital. It was a transcendent event that transported the audience beyond music itself to a mystical experience —just as Scriabin intended.

Rachmanov Plays Tchaikovsky

Dmitry Rachmanov's recent recording of the piano music of Pyotr Tchaikovsky is certainly a cause for celebration. First and foremost is the world class playing, abounding in virtuosity and authentic insights. Second there is the feeling of discovery. Even though Tchaikovsky is one of the most popular composers on the concert stage today—just think of the last three symphonies, the *Violin Concerto*, the *First Piano Concerto*, the *Swan Lake* and *Nutcracker Ballet* music, *Romeo and Juliet* and *1812 Overtures*—his compositions for solo piano are less well known, at least in the United States. Rachmanov's CD goes a long way to remedy this situation.

A first time listener is struck by the cosmopolitan, "classical" outlook of the music: no Wagnerisms here! The music may not be overtly nationalistic, yet it sounds distinctly Russian, especially the soulful *Dumka,* which creates a convincing blend of folk song and bravura.

The *Six Piano Pieces, op. 19* and the *Two Pieces, op. 10* display a variety of moods from tender melancholy to spontaneous gaiety. Amid the charming melodies and inventive figurations, Rachmanov is persuasive in identifying the various characters of the music, especially in the last piece of *Op. 19*, a substantial theme and variations that can stand as an independent concert work.

The *Grand Sonata in G Major, op. 37* is a kind of symphony for solo piano. Its massive chordal textures and driving rhythms create a theatrical effect. In this work as in all the others, Rachmanov commands a full range of color and nuance. The recorded sound of the Steinway piano has "presence" and the right amount of reverberation. The lucid program notes are by the pianist himself.

At seventy-nine minutes, this impressive disc offers a generous sampling of music by a beloved Russian master performed by a master Russian pianist. It is a valuable contribution to our appreciation of Romantic repertory.

Part II
Rememberings

Charles' influence was memorable to composers, colleagues, students and audiences that came into his orbit. They provide a glimpse into the importance of his influence on them.

Françoise Regnat
My Friend and Colleague

I first met Charles in 1972 when I began teaching at California State University, Northridge. He had already been there for two years and was very courteous and supportive to me as a new faculty member. My first impression of him was that of a quiet person, very measured in the way he spoke and he always got to the point.

Charles was an excellent piano teacher but he was also a scholar, he had a very analytic mind. His students got so much more than pianistic technical information from their lessons or attending his master classes. They received insight into the context in which the piece was written, details about the composer and the time period. Charles would ignite his students' curiosity and make them think.

At the end of each semester we sat on students' juries and provided comments about each student's performance. He never went on long tirades but what he had to say was always meaningful and right on target.

Of course, we all knew that he was very good at communicating his thoughts in writing. He wrote countless thoroughly researched articles for various publications. Personally, I looked forward to reading the program notes he wrote for his recitals on campus and always learned something. I may still have some of them at home!

When I first met him, Charles was playing mainly twentieth-century repertoire, but of composers whose pieces were not familiar to me at that time. I am thinking of Copland and Hindemith in particular. But he also performed very contemporary repertoire, such as George Crumb's

Makrokosmos, and I have to thank him for opening up my ears to that repertoire.

We played a few concerts together. Early on I remember a performance of the Bartok *Sonata for Two Pianos and Percussion.* More recently, in our older age, we did the Hindemith *Sonata for Piano Four Hands.* I went to his house to rehearse a few times. We had fun. He asked one of his neighbors to come and listen to us in our dress rehearsal!

After he retired from teaching at CSUN, Charles kept busy, always working on some projects. There was less twentieth-century music in his recital programs. He embarked on performing several recitals of Beethoven sonatas and I also remember a recital where he gave a masterful performance of Brahms' *Handel Variations.* It didn't matter if he was playing for a small group of people, a music teachers' gathering or a large faculty recital, he wanted to keep practicing, playing and performing. For several months before his death he had been working on the *Sonata for Piano and Violin* by Guillaume Lekeu. This composer was his latest discovery. He was raving about the piece, telling me how beautiful it was and how much he was looking forward to performing it. He played it with violinist Jacqueline Suzuki at a noon concert soon after. He was eager to perform in future concerts the Lekeu *Piano Trio* and *Piano Quartet.* Unfortunately that never happened.

Françoise Regnat: concert soloist and collaborative artist, Professor Emeritus of Music at California State University, Northridge.

Kristi Lobitz
An Adjudicator of the Highest Degree

I met Dr. Charles Fierro when I was a student at California State University, Northridge where I studied with Polish Artist-in-Residence, Jakob Gimpel. At that time, although I was steeped in the repertoire of Chopin, Bach, Czerny, Cramer and the European masters; I was also aware of Charles' reputation as a fabulous pianist who specialized in the contemporary piano repertory. However, I had no first-hand experience with his pianistic skills until I turned pages for him years later when he played Hindemith's *Ludus Tonalis* on a local Los Angeles music series. Needless to say after that performance, he had all my respect.

I became reacquainted with Charles when I served as State Chair for the MTAC Piano Concerto and Solo Competition for nearly a decade. I engaged nine judges every year for the various categories, and Charles, like so many here in the Southland, quickly became one of my favorites.

He was knowledgeable about all kinds of piano literature, a first-class gentleman and possessed a native curiosity about people, including me. He was always interested in hearing what I was doing in my professional life as a pianist, professor and competition chair! So, it was not difficult to connect personally with Charles. He also had many interesting things to say about the subject of music in general and frequent thoughtful opinions to share.

As a judge/adjudicator of piano competitions, Charles captured the essence of a performance in a nutshell which usually consisted of a short paragraph with four to five sentences. He was articulate in his comments and wrote in an eloquent, expressive and succinct style. Reading his remarks, I was impressed by the accuracy with which he summed up a performance, as well as the kindness he showed toward the students he was judging. There was even a gracefulness in his handwriting!

About the fourth Chopin *Ballade*, he wrote: "Shows natural flexibility of delivery and insight into the music in all its varied aspects. Beautiful tone throughout, sensitive playing and artistic tempo management." If I had been a young competitor, I would have walked out of the competition on a cloud.

It wasn't Charles' style to tear down a student but rather to affirm good playing and tactfully correct playing that hadn't yet arrived. About Messiaen's *Vingt Regards sur L'Enfant Jesus*, he wrote: "The challenge in '*La Parole*' is to make the sound interesting even when given an unvarying dynamic indication. '*Noel*' shows a more varied array of metallic coloration in the playing. In both pieces, the art of listening is paramount. Use imagination. Very promising performance, with much courage."

This same vein of commentary continued for another student who happened to be playing Liszt's *Un Sospiro*: "Well played, although I missed a sense of 'romance' and spontaneous poetry. Cultivate imagination. Think about the music as coming from your own life experience." Charles understood the art of encouragement.

His writing also belied a probing, intelligent mind that revealed itself in a highly descriptive style. His review of a student playing Liszt's *Rhapsodie Espagnole* went like this: "A personal interpretation of this piece, in the best sense of the word. It had color, fire, charm, surprise, humor, grandeur. The slow parts, in particular, sounded quite Spanish. The passagework sparkled."

Finally, students who played modern masterworks were terribly lucky to get feedback from Charles, given his experience studying and researching the genre. About Scriabin's *Black Mass Sonata,* he wrote: "Intelligent performance, tempo and mood changes. Sound sensitivity is very important in this piece; go for infinite varieties of *piano* and *pianissimo,* and imaginative pedal; the pounding passage should sound [more] violent."

And responding to a performance of the Berg *Sonata* he offered: "Projection of the outward (constructive) details of this piece was well done; you may want to consider the inward content; what this piece is really about, the personal anguish, the extreme sensitivity, doubt and collapse of the culture it comes from."

To summarize, the presence of Charles Fierro on a performance panel or jury was a competition chair's dream. Having him there as a sage, experienced judge always eased some of the stress for me, and I relaxed knowing that accurate commentary and fair decisions would emerge at the end of the day. My world also opened up a little as a result of hearing his enlightened performance of the Hindemith cycle. I realized that Charles had made his mark not only on me but on the entire Southern California musical community as well.

Kristi Lobitz: pianist, faculty member Loyola Marymount University, Pasadena City College, El Camino College, Chair, Concerto-Solo Competition Music Teachers' Association of California (2007-2016), Southern California Junior Bach Festival, Region II Chair.

Sachiko Kato
Hello Dr. Fierro?
"Saa-chi-i-i-ko-o-o!"

Dr. Fierro always picked up my calls from New York with genuine excitement in his voice, which always made me feel he was happy to hear from me and welcomed the conversation. Of course this made me happy too. He was one of few people I was able to open up to and with whom I could talk about anything. And he told me to call him "Charles," because now I was his equal, but I kept calling him "Dr. Fierro" because I felt uncomfortable calling my former professor by his first name due to my stubbornly-rooted Japanese formality, even though I have lived in the United States for decades now.

Although Dr. Fierro was not my private teacher at California State University, Northridge (CSUN), he was one of very few people who played an influential role in my life and career. I had his Piano Literature (a sort of master class) every Friday afternoon for at least a couple of years during my study at CSUN. At the time, I was under tremendous pressure facing the dilemma of whether to pursue a career in music or stay home to help my parents, who were going through financial struggles.

Yes, I wanted to be a pianist. I won quite a few local competitions and wanted to try my talent on the bigger stage in New York. But my parents were on the verge of bankruptcy and they wanted me to keep helping them at their restaurant. My father even told me that music is something rich kids do, and I was certainly not a rich kid. He said, "What is a poor man's daughter doing playing the piano?" I chose CSUN because of the proximity and low tuition and because my parents didn't care what I did as long as they didn't have to pay the tuition and I kept helping them out at the restaurant. But I wanted to go to New York City to try to see how far my talent might take me. So I kept asking myself: "Should I pursue my ambition and dream instead of taking care of my parents? But isn't it selfish of me to abandon my hapless parents?"

I found a sympathetic listener in Dr. Fierro. I stayed behind after his class one day and explained my dilemma and ended up breaking down and crying furiously. I am pretty sure I am the first one who broke down in front of him not just once, but twice (I had the similar episode a few months later). Dr. Fierro told me in a calming manner that he thinks I have what it takes and I should pursue what I want.

As luck would have it, I would end up in New York, having been accepted to Juilliard for graduate study, and then having managed to graduate with the help of financial aid and multiple part-time jobs. It was then that our periodic phone conversations began. He was there every time, happy to receive my calls, always listening with great interest, encouraging and advising me as I struggled to "make it" both in terms of my musical career and financially, trying to find my true self in the process.

And suddenly he has passed away.

I am now probably at the same age as or even older than Dr. Fierro was when I first met him. After so many years of struggle, I now have a flourishing teaching studio here in New York City as well as three CDs and have just written and published a piano method book. I want to tell him that not only have I survived in New York, but against all odds, and with his kind encouragement, I have found my own niche in this competitive field.

I would call him by his first name now if I could talk to him again.

"Charles! I have quite a few serious students whom I enjoy teaching! I want to become the teacher and the friend you were with me, with my students, continuing to welcome, encourage and inspire them even after they leave me just like you did. Charles, I have finally arrived where I aspired to be all those years ago. Thank you for your encouragement for all these decades!"

Sachiko Kato: concert pianist, recording artist, piano pedagogue, author: The Sachiko Method: How to Find the Music Within You.

Jan Sanborn
My Dear Friend and Mentor

In the late '80s, after raising five children, touring in musical groups, involvement in various church music programs, I turned toward finishing my own college degree. California State Univeristy, Northridge was in the vicinity, and its music department had a great reputation.

Off I went, to audition to receive piano lessons. I intended to study with a faculty member who, as it turned out, preferred younger students with longer careers ahead of them. I was bereft.

Then I was introduced to Dr. Charles Fierro, who graciously consented to take me as a student. It became apparent that I was fortunate to work with one of the best piano professors anywhere. Dr. Fierro had a complete knowledge of the instrument, of the literature, of technique, of the sociological events surrounding each composition. He invested of himself in each student, and I was a blessed recipient of that investment. He cared deeply about our performances, and always promoted them to all.

His master classes were legendary, and when we finished a session we had been given thorough knowledge of the substance and intent of each piece. He made the music come alive, vital and exciting.

We became fast friends, and even after his retirement, as he continued to share with the musical community, I kept learning from him. We lost a great one when he passed away, but I will forever be thankful for the hours well spent sharing the joy of music with my dear friend and mentor, Dr. Charles Fierro.

Jan Sanborn: pianist and published composer, Fred Bock Music Group and Alfred Publishing.

Jon Sakata
So Many Glimpses

One of the great joys when on the piano faculty at New England Conservatory was the opportunity to invite Charles to perform and lecture on Aaron Copland's *Piano Fantasy* at the Conservatory. Of many memorable exchanges that took place during his visit, one that remains most vivid was when he and the pioneering composer/theorist Robert Cogan reminisced about their respective interactions with Copland. Cogan told the story of when he was in the composition seminar at Tanglewood being given that summer by Copland: specifically, the day Copland arrived at the seminar with a new recording in hand, yet to be publicly released but sent to him by the composer. Copland prefaced playing the recording to the attendees by saying: "While we may each be writing in diverse styles and musical languages and may hold preference for one school of composition over another, it is important that we engage with works of consequence, which I think the piece I wish to play for you shortly, certainly is. It isn't a matter of whether you like or dislike this piece; but it is imperative that you engage with it directly and form a long-term relationship with it … whatever that may be." The work that Copland shared with them that day was Elliott Carter's first *String Quartet*.

After Charles had returned to Los Angeles, we spoke on the phone. We reminded him of this exchange and expressed the following: "Charles, what Bob mentioned about his seminar with Copland and the importance of not only encountering 'new' music but forming 'long-term relationship(s)' with works is something we took centrally away from our studies with you. As you know, our careers as performers, from working with Cage just before his death to premiering works written for us around the globe, truly is part of a trajectory and arc that originated from our studies with you. And not only to the extent of our performing these 'new' pieces as some sort of field of specialization but how this has shaped how we engage and interpret ALL music. As you used to say to us: ALL music is contemporary music because we're playing it right now!"

With Charles' passing Jung Mi and I are left with so many glimpses – some visual but mostly auditory. After our studies with him in the late '80s, the past three decades have been a deep friendship that, while including memorable occasions of being in one another's company, has largely consisted of our regular multi-hour phone conversations. The trajectories and arc of our lives have been so indelibly marked by our studies with him; but perhaps even more so, over these many years, by the profound longitude and latitude of these conversations. His teaching and nurturing continued but also his own sense of (ad)venture, curiosity, learning, desire to expand his (and our) horizons in artistic challenge, potentialization and complexification.

One of the projects of ours that gave Charles immense pleasure and provided such a rich reservoir for our talks was a collaborative project we did with a team of architects based in Boston for the fortieth anniversary of Phillips Exeter Academy's Class of '45 Library designed by Louis Kahn. The video collage played for Charles' tribute concert was a favorite of his and featured our performance of Cogan's *Contexts Memories: Version C (2000) for two pianos*. This work is itself a memory, or series of memories, of an earlier composition by Cogan called *Algebra and Mornings* (a collection of solo piano studies) where now fragments/fractures of the earlier set are remembered, overlaid, intersected, collided with one another. The video, like the music, eschews memory as sentimental souvenir or nostalgia; but rather poses it as a force of destabilization, vertigo, unleashed creative potency and power. Like our studies and conversations with Charles, the duo and the video embody a dynamic assemblage where the immensity and range of ideas, energies, relations are ever increasingly widened and intensified. Precisely, as we and Charles used to talk about: what Spinoza called Joy.

Jon Sakata: concert soloist and transdisciplinary artisan, faculty Phillips Exeter Academy.

Afterthoughts II

Master Teacher

Charles was a favorite master teacher at the Sara Compinsky Master Class year after year. Performers and auditors alike received valuable insight from his critiques and suggestions as remembered by class participants.

Reflections from Sara Compinsky Master Class

As a frequent leader of the Sara Compinsky Master Class, Charles Fierro always inspired us with his story telling and his vast knowledge and understanding of the historical elements and how that can help us understand and interpret the music. His gentle encouragement was highly valued by the class members. We miss him and will always appreciate his special gifts that helped us to grow as pianists and musicians.

—Noëlle Compinsky Tinturin

Gleanings from a Master Class with Dr. Fierro

What do you hope to take away from a master class? Performers and listeners alike have the high expectation of gaining expert technical knowledge, insightful recommendations, creative ideas and at the end of class, the desire to rush home to practice. A master teacher has big shoes to fill. In addition to knowing the repertoire inside and out and being able to perform it, he/she must have full knowledge of the composer and the cultural attitude of the times. Music is written by real people in challenging times and acquainting us with their lives and experiences offers incentive to dig deeper, find out more and apply our findings to our musical studies.

Dr. Charles Fierro offers all of the above in his master classes. We reap the reward of his thirty years of experience as professor of piano at California State University, Northridge and his extensive and noteworthy performances and recording accomplishments. In addition, his ability to communicate years of scholarly research into interesting and understandable presentations has made him a sought-after master class teacher.

I recall a master class in which three pieces from *Romeo and Juliet* by Prokofiev were performed. Dr. Fierro explained that the music is a transcription of orchestral ballet music and we should always be thinking of orchestral instruments when playing it. Studying the orchestral score will be very helpful to get ideas about the color and variety in the music. He went on to say that Prokofiev was constantly coming up with melodies, and they were always tonal. Even though Prokofiev lived at the time of Schoenberg, he felt there was more potential in the tonal system than in the twelve-tone system. Within his melodies he was quick to change keys and his rhythms are in constant motion. Prokofiev had the ability to be modern within a traditional system.

In another class a Rachmaninoff concerto was performed and Dr. Fierro mentioned that he had recently seen a photograph of Rachmaninoff sitting at his piano and there was a metronome perched on top. This tells us that within his great romanticism and deep emotionalism, Rachmaninoff gave attention to time and tempo. He wrote metronome markings in most of his scores and he meant for us to follow them.

The sonatas of Scarlatti were discussed in another class. It is interesting to note that Scarlatti lived at the exact time of Bach and Handel but he didn't have any contact with them. No pictures exist of Scarlatti and we remember him mostly for the sonatas he composed later in life. He was a brilliant harpsichordist and became the harpsichord teacher of the Queen of Spain. He was constantly writing sonatas and drew inspiration from Italian opera, gypsy music, flamenco dance, church music and chamber music. His ideas were unique and inexhaustible but the form of his sonatas was not original—most of them have a split in the middle and each half is repeated. Scarlatti is much more of a comprehensive and universal composer than he is known for but we need to listen to many of his sonatas to recognize this. There is an excellent recording of the complete Scarlatti sonatas by Scott Ross for listeners who want to dig deeper into the depths of Scarlatti's music.

Most recently, thirteen year old Benjamin Krasner performed the Chopin *Concerto in E Minor,* second and third movements in a master class. Dr. Fierro's suggestion to listeners was that in our playing we should carry forward the fearlessness of youth into adulthood. When we mature we become aware of so many things that create excessive caution; is it too loud, too fast, is the pedal right? When we are young we have no concerns like that, we just do it. That's the ideal state of divinely inspired music. We learn the music in our wisdom but we should play it with fearlessness like young people.

When playing a long piece, Dr. Fierro suggested making a map. Concertos, long sonatas, fantasies and rondos are often complicated with many sections, sub-sections and transitions. We must always know where we are going and by blocking out the harmonic sections, thematic sections, transitions and returns we can see the whole structure of the piece. This is called having a synoptic view. We tend to be more familiar with a diachronic view of a piece which includes all things related to time. We go through the piece in detail and consider *rubato*, contrasts, direction, expression and tempo, among other things. Ideally, when practicing we should consider both of these views.

To observe a skilled master teacher work with a talented student is like watching a sculptor mold a piece of clay. Both contain the raw material for the creation of a masterpiece.

—Mary A. Hannon

Charles' map of the Prokofiev Toccata

Conclusion

Interview with Nancy Fierro by Mary A. Hannon

Charles Fierro In His Own Words concludes with the editor's interview of Nancy Fierro, Charles' sister, who shares with us her unique perspective on her brother's life and career.

How early did Charles display his talent?

Charles was gifted in music from the start. When he was a boy, my dad used to play what I thought was a fun game with him. He would have him face the wall with his back to the piano. Then dad played various notes and asked him to identify them. I thought it was magic that Charles could name every one of them perfectly. We both took pianos lessons, each starting at age six. He, as my older brother, ahead of me. We were both enthusiastic about lessons and with one piano in the house, we frequently fought over who was to practice the first. One day when I was practicing and he was mowing the lawn outside, he shouted, "You are playing an F and it's supposed to be an F-sharp!"

How did his career start?

In the 1960s, Charles attended USC School of Music and while there studied piano with some of the finest professors in America—Lillian Steuber, Johanna Graudan. He became a close friend of composer Ingolf Dahl who was on the faculty there and they sometimes hiked together in the mountains. At graduation, he was awarded a Doctor of Music with distinction. With the support of his mentors, he went on to become a leading pianist in California.

After teaching at Pierce College for a few years, Charles held a post as professor of music at California State University, Northridge for thirty years. His students always spoke of him as an engaging and brilliant instructor who could clearly communicate his insights with ease. A devoted and caring teacher, he inquired about their well-being long after they left his studio. Cards and letters from them, which Charles kept in his personal files, express respect, gratitude, admiration and affection for their teacher. He always thought carefully about how best to educate each student according to their individual abilities and talents.

Despite the demands of being a fulltime professor, Charles continued to perform nationally and internationally, make recordings, write articles, give master classes and adjudicate competitions. After giving his first concert in France at the Fontainebleau Palace, Nadia Boulanger commented that his performance displayed "most musical understanding and masterly technique." Music teachers' organizations sought after him for his insightful lecture-recitals and master classes and because they valued his perceptive and encouraging adjudications.

You are a professional pianist too. How did Charles influence you as musician?

Before giving concerts, Charles and I would often engage in long conversation about the music we were preparing to play and the implications the score might have on interpretation and expression. We would run through our pieces for each other over the phone—sharing our perspective of what we heard. He graciously accepted any critical suggestions I might offer. And when he remarked on my playing, he would pinpoint any artistic problem yet to be solved or pose questions to goad me on to discover what more I could find and say in my interpretation. I imagined this was the way he taught his students. Although Charles preferred playing solo, I once invited him to perform duo piano with me to give the West Coast Premiere of Grażyna Bacewicz's *Concerto for Two Pianos*. We performed this together with Mozart's *Concerto in E-Flat Major K.365* both with the Ventura Symphony Orchestra, Frank Salazar conducting. Charles composed lively cadenzas for us and we got good reviews from the press who spotlighted the novelty of a brother-sister piano team.

How would you describe Charles' influence on the Los Angeles music scene in his day?

Charles was a well-known pianist in the Los Angeles musical scene. I attended most of his concerts in town. I remember he was a regular performer at the Los Angeles Monday Evening Concerts and often gave premieres of contemporary works at the summer Ojai festivals. He exchanged letters with musical giants of the day—Aaron Copland, George Crumb, William Schuman, Carlos Chavez, John Corigliano. His repertoire encompassed a wide variety of periods and styles. He felt musicians should not confine themselves to performing familiar figures in the listeners' "Musical

Pantheon" as he called it. He aired works he felt should be brought to audience attention: Purcell, Byrd, Lekeu, MacDowell. At the same time, he devoted himself to the performance and study of the traditional repertoire. He was recognized for his original insights into the music of Beethoven, Schumann and Liszt.

Charles never shied away from music that was intellectually or technically demanding: Copland's *Piano Fantasy*, George Hummel's *The Universe*. But the work that drew his keen interest was Paul Hindemith's hour-long piano solo *Ludus Tonalis*. Charles once told me that of all the music he played the *Ludus Tonalis* was the closest to his heart. He first became acquainted with this piece when he was in his twenties and for the next fifty years, he continued to mine its wonders.

How would you summarize Charles' role as a mentor?

I would like to answer that question by sharing a little about Hindemith's *Ludus Tonalis* because Charles loved it so much and because as he once said "what we play says as much about us as how we play it."

As you may know, *Ludus Tonalis* is Latin for "Play or Game of Tones." Hindemith wrote this work in 1942. The music is made up of twenty-five distinct pieces—prelude, interludes, fugues and postlude that relate to each other and to the unified whole in a cohesive construction unique to Hindemith's view of tonal organization. There are no "virtuosic displays" in this grand work, "only pure music" as Charles noted. The music begins in C, explores keys tonally and chromatically related through its overtones, and then ends in C. Altogether, the twenty-five pieces combine to form a magnificent arc—a tour de force of compositional skill and artistic beauty.

For Hindemith, *Ludus Tonalis* in its vast comprehension symbolized and expressed nothing less than the harmonious order of the universe. It is visionary, complex yet accessible, playful "*Ludus*" and according to Hindemith's philosophy, morally uplifting in intent. These are sublime qualities that I believe informed Charles' philosophy of his performances and teaching as well as his life's trajectory. My teacher, Nadia Boulanger, once remarked that people with an inner life and the means to exteriorize it are rare. I truly believe Charles was one of those exceptional human beings.

Photo Credits

Aaron Copland and Charles—SavageMind/Quinn. Used with permission of Delos Records.

Ingold Dahl—USC Libraries Special Collections (Ingolf Dahl). Used with permission.

Edward MacDowell—Photograph of Edward MacDowell: this was published in Hagedorn, Hermann (December 28, 1921). "The Peterborough Colony". The Outlook 129 (17): 688. New York, United States: The Outlook Company. Retrieved on October 18, 2011. Copyright: Public Domain.

Paul Hindemith—Foto vom Hindemith-Institutals Rechteinhaber unter GFDL zur Verfügung gestellt Hochgeladen nach de.wikipedia von de:Benutzer:Axel.

Arnold Schoenberg—photo by Florence Homolka believed to be taken in Los Angeles, 1948. The Schoenberg Archives at USC grants permission to publish this image.

Guillaume Lekeu—Photo by Studio, Emile Rat, Poitiers. Bibliotheque National de France, 1886. Copyright: Public Domain.

Charles Fierro Scholarship Endowment

Charles Fierro's family, friends and students wanted to continue his legacy of excellence, dedication and support for the education of piano students at California State University, Northridge where he taught for thirty years. To accomplish this goal, they established The Charles Fierro Piano Scholarship Endowment together with the University Development Office. The Endowment currently provides financial assistance to talented students pursuing a degree in piano performance. It is a small beginning; and as the Endowment grows, more and more students will be able to benefit. If you wish to make a donation in honor of Dr. Fierro, please call the Director of Development at (818) 677-4269. Thank you!

Links

Charles Fierro Copland Music

Charles Fierro performs Ludus Tonalis at CSUN in 2012

MacDowell: Eroica Sonata, 12 Etudes/Charles Fierro

Charles Fierro MacDowell First Modern Suite/Sonata 4

Edward MacDowell, Charles Fierro—Piano Music Vol. II: Woodland Sketches, Sea Pieces

Charles Fierro Recordings on Apple Music

Nancy Fierro—Charles Fierro YouTube Channel

www.ingramcontent.com/pod-product-compliance
Ingram Content Group UK Ltd.
Pitfield, Milton Keynes, MK11 3LW, UK
UKHW020225250726
13967UKWH00001B/186

9 780578 958606